I'M TELLING

I'm Telling

Confessions of a
Middle-Aged Middle-Class Mother

by

Dolores Curran

EMMAUS
BOOKS
PAULIST PRESS

Library of Congress
Catalog Card Number: 77-14822

ISBN: 0-8091-2073-9

Published by Paulist Press
Editorial Office: 1865 Broadway, New York, N.Y. 10023
Business Office: 545 Island Road, Ramsey, N.J. 07446

Printed and bound in the
United States of America

Contents

Dedicated to
my sisters-in-law:
    Joan
    JoAnne
    Kathy
    Mary
    Mary Lynn

I
On Being a Perfect Parent

I didn't think I could ever be a perfect parent. Oh, I tried. I read the books and applied the principles and changed my tactics every three days, but my children still fought. They also fibbed, lifted cookies and looked me straight in the eye and said, "Because I don't want to wear boots."

I went through all the anguish of aspiring Perfect Parents. I looked at that sweet dumpling of a first baby in the hospital nursery and vowed that I would be the ideal mother, never scolding, complaining or despairing. I didn't realize then how easy it was to be all those things when someone else was taking care of the children.

Anyway, for years I was not the Perfect Parent. In fact, I got used to being the imperfect parent, thrusting out my forefinger at an impertinent face, saying "Because I said so!" I figured that if the children didn't have to be rational, neither did I, so I wasn't. What's more, I didn't even ask who did it, I just accused. It was quicker and, percentages being what they are, I hit the culprit right one-third of the time.

My children got used to my being imperfect, and I think they rather liked me that way. They respected my system of injustice and irrationality and I respected theirs. It was a case of imperfect meets imperfect.

Then I met a Perfect Parent. It was like being thrown off a horse. I had been looking at the whole thing wrong. I thought the Perfect Parent had to have Perfect Children. Not true, I discovered.

This Perfect Parent told our group how to be perfect while her children trod on our insteps and rifled our purses. She explained to us that all we had to do was tell our children the right way to do things and our responsibility was ended. If they didn't behave after that, it wasn't our fault. We had fulfilled our obligations as Perfect Parents.

I was delighted. I felt like Ponce de Leon discovering the fountain of sanity. I could have my crown and my children, too. I went home and began telling my children the right way to do things.

"Eat neatly," I said at dinner, righteously fulfilling my responsibility in teaching decent table manners. I didn't say a word when one dunked his bread into his milk or even flinch when one dumped his milk in my lap. I smiled graciously, like the Perfect Parent I was. After dinner, I chucked the tablecloth in the garbage can and began to shovel out under the table.

"Dress Neatly," I said the next morning, quickly disposing of my responsibility in getting the children off to school. One child wore a sweatshirt and leotards, while another combined denim and lace. I smiled and suggested that if anyone asked them their last name, they were to say, "Johnson."

Perfect Parenthood went well for about three days, and then the house began looking like the kids' rooms. I began to worry that being a Perfect Parent was going to be rather hard on being a Perfect Housekeeper.

A week or so and a couple of phone calls later suggested that my children weren't perfect neighbors. I explained to my geographical friends that I had told them not to ride their bikes over newly cultivated gardens but that didn't seem to help reassure the neighbors any.

Well, a few other things happened, and as you've probably suspected by now, I discovered that Perfect Parenthood wasn't for me. The kids began to crack under the strain.

"How come you're smiling so much instead of yelling?" one asked. They were all waiting for me to explode over their messiness and misbehavior.

When did it happen? Yesterday, and it was perfectly marvelous. My perfect bare foot picked up a jack as soon as I stepped out of bed. That was just the beginning. The toothbrushes had been used for screen painting and the good sheets for monster caves.

My Perfect Temper snapped when I saw my kids and my house. It was just a short but beautiful trip back to imperfect parenthood. And when we got through picking up and scrubbing, I was doing the screaming and the kids were smiling.

"Gee, Mom, it's good to have you back again," said one child, nursing a smarting knuckle I gave him for something his brother did. But who cared? We were imperfect again.

II
<u>This</u> Is the Day
the Lord Hath Made?

One of my favorite posters depicts a tired and cranky toddler with a bowl of spaghetti turned upside down on his head. Underneath the caption reads, "This is the day that the Lord hath made; rejoice and be glad in it."

I had that picture hanging in my kitchen for a long time and it gave me much sustenance. Then I gave it to my sister-in-law, mother of eight, and I wasn't surprised to see it hanging in her kitchen the last time I was there.

Sometimes Scripture gets a bit lofty for the ordinary day and it's good to put it into perspective. Any parent has dozens of days with children who look like that cranky spaghetti eater (or decorator, if you prefer) and it's foolish to pretend that we get anywhere near rejoicing over them.

Popular religious literature would have us believe that the good Christian parent never loses her/his temper. Nonsense. It takes a sturdy parent to even look at that poster, not to mention living with it daily.

Religious tracts on parenthood often paint the good mother as ever sweet, compliant and smiling as she wipes up the milk which has dripped through the crack in the table onto her Supphose. Never, anywhere, have I read a prayer surrounding a good loud down-to-earth mother tantrum. That's because we aren't supposed to

4

have them, just as we aren't supposed to have children who turn bowls of spaghetti upside down on their heads.

Well, we have them, plenty of them. When we're in a rush to get to Little League Liturgy and four kids are fighting for the one seat by the window, we don't smile sweetly and suggest a family summit conference. We shout, "Move over," and glare at the squatter who spends the rest of the day pouting. (Rejoice and be glad in it?)

When we pull out a sheet of 100 thirteen-cent stamps and discover that a son has used them to practice rubber stamping on, we don't praise his creativity and patiently explain that he just canceled $13 worth of stamps. We scream irrational things about allowances, carelessness, and maybe even a hint of stupidity. (Rejoice and be glad in it?)

When we spend hours on a family activity, like camping or crafting, only to hear the children say, "I wish we could watch TV instead," we're apt to blow our halos. At that moment we don't gaze fondly upon our fruit of the vine and pray that they continue to multiply like olive branches. Rather, we get tight-lipped, or we shout, or cry.

The children, however, have their problems with rejoicing, too. On the last Feast of the Holy Family, ours wasn't, so in a burst of parental impatience we sent them to bed earlier than usual. When we got ready for bed later, we found on our pillow this carefully disguised excerpt from that morning's Gospel, "You who are wives, be submissive to your husbands. *And fathers, do not nag your children lest they lose heart.*"

What did we do? We laughed to the point of exhaustion, truly rejoicing in that day the Lord had made.

5

III
Dropping Out
of Breakfast

About the only advantage to breakfast is that it comes early in the day. The trauma, cleanup and tears are usually over in time for Mom to get ready for lunch. Lunch is much better. There are fewer kids, they are tired and there's no choice over the brand of peanut butter.

To be fair, I admit some women like breakfast. I know one. She eats on a lace tablecloth and puts her jelly in a crystal dish without label. After placing an insulated pot of coffee next to her plate, she munches her toast appreciatively as she reads the *Saturday Review*. She has no children.

For women like her, and for husbands who take the cowardly way out of facing their heirs at the daily oatmeal scrimmage, let me tell it like it is.

There's nothing more appalling to a nearly awake parent than a kitchen full of over-sleepy, over-hungry kids bent on beating each other to the cereal premium. No matter which six boxes of cereal you line up, they will be the wrong ones.

The level of the breakfast discussion?

"He gots 16 raisins and I only gots 11 in my cereal."

"Ronnie poured grape juice in my milk."

"No, Jenny, you should only put two spoons of sugar on that sugared cereal."

"How come there's milk dripping through that crack in the table?"

If breakfast ends—and this is a sure sign of the goodness of God—there's still the battle over cereal box coupons and cutouts. If we mothers had any energy left at all, we would boycott all cereal manufacturers until they came out with a solid-color, no-print box.

My list of cereal producers to be attacked:

—Those whose illustration of premiums dwarfs the tiny plastic prize itself, bringing tears of disappointment to sugar-flaked faces. This same serenity-spoiler adds the indignity of making mother admit she can't assemble the stamped plastic bomber. By the time Dad comes home, it is broken, of course.

—Those who write a big FREE right above the words, "for only five coupons and fifty cents."

—Those who print puppets, paper dolls and puzzles on the boxes themselves. I once tried to store dry cereal in a box so riddled by little scissors I didn't even have to pour it out. I just swept it from the shelf into bowls.

—Those who print offers and cartoons on both sides of the box so two kids facing each other can get into a revolving fight.

—Those who give their products ridiculous names like Oatsy Doats and Funny Honies. It's bad enough for an adult to endure the humiliation of breakfast without having to sound like a three-year-old, "Okay, Jenny, do you want Bear Hugs, Mustacchios, or Big Toes?"

I've never understood why educators haven't capitalized on cereal box reading lessons since they are easily the most well-read material in the home. I visualize a box reading: See the cereal. It is good. Eat the cereal. Do not throw the cereal. Do not spill the milk. Do not laugh. Do not fight. Eat, eat, eat.

I could go on, but it is too painful.

I know one mother who escaped it, though. Last year when her husband told her he was giving up breakfast for Lent, she exploded, "Oh no you don't. You've pulled that the past three years. This year it's my turn."

And she had a perfectly marvelous Lent.

IV
I've Got a Little List

Once one of Beth's teachers saw an article of mine in print and asked her how I happened to start writing. "Oh, I dunno," replied our totally-unimpressed firstborn. "I guess it's because she writes lists all the time."

When the teacher reported it to me later, I winced, making a mental note to put it on my "writing list." That time has come.

I would feel better if I knew other women made lists, too. I've been teased about the number and variety of my lists so incessantly by fellow teachers, husband, children, and friends that I'm beginning to wonder if I am a listomaniac, or whatever it is they call list addicts.

Some of my lists are tacked to the bulletin board above my desk, some to the kitchen bulletin board. Others can be found in such intriguing spots as mirrors, old purses, and the junk drawer. The invention of those marvelous magnetic daisies makes every appliance a listing nest. I keep lists of untried recipes tacked to the range, lists of uneaten leftovers tacked to the refrigerator, and unmatched socks tacked to the washer.

My lists fall into categories, and they were proving a little unwieldy, so I've made a Master List of Lists. Here it is.

FAMILY LISTS
Grocery list
Immunization list
We exposed list
We were exposed by list
Allowance taken away list
etc.

PERSONAL LISTS
Baby-sitting owed list
Invite to dinner list
Birthday party list
Changing size list
etc.

WRITING LISTS
Idea lists
Mss. overdue list
Mss. way-overdue list
Editor lost interest list
Fan mail list
Nasty fan mail list
etc.

MISCELLANEOUS
Dress hem lists (down, no, now up)
Closets to clean list
Books to write list
Vacations to go on list
etc.

These are just my own lists. I make others for my husband and kids. On Jim's list, there are homey little items like: glue playpen; write home; fix can-opener; write home about playpen, etc. ("When you have a writer for a wife," he tells friends, "she nags *in writing*.")

I can't imagine any woman operating without lists,

but I understand that some do. They seem to operate a little more efficiently than I do. Maybe it's because it takes me so long to write my lists. Right now, I'm thinking of ways to speed up my list-writing. So far, here's what I have:

LIST-SPEEDING LIST

1. Cut down on number of lists
2. Read lists only once a week
3. Abrvate whn psble
4. Make list of abbreviations
5. Etc.

V
Order in the Pew!

It begins at home every Sunday morning. "Do you have your money for the collection basket?"

"Yeah."

"Yup."

"Uh huh."

"Where?" I ask.

"Where what?" they reply

"Where are you keeping your collection money?"

"In my hand," replies one.

"In my purse," replies another.

The third points to his sneaker.

I launch into the familiar, ". . . how many times do I have to tell you . . . a safe place to keep it . . . if it drops, it stays on the floor . . ."

It continues in the car. "*Today*, I don't want to have to glare at a single child, understand?"

They nod. They understand, but one asks, "What's glare mean?"

"Glare is the kind of look I give you when you interrupt my prayers to ask how much longer Mass is going to be or some other question."

"Oh, glare is a church look."

My husband changes the direction but not the subject of the conversation. "At Communion time, Mike and Steve are to sit quietly until we get back. Understand?

No more pew sliding or kneeler banging or giggling . . ."

"We didn't bang the kneelers last time. They . . ."

"Never mind. We went through all that last week. Just remember what happened last week."

"Ooookay."

Three minutes out for recollection and pouting.

It continues in the vestibule. Whispering now. "Steve, I want to hear a good clear Our Father from you."

It continues down the aisle. "A good genuflection, now."

It continues in the pew. "No, Sara has to go first. Then me." We can't put two children next to each other, heaven forbid.

It continues through the Weekly Missalette Grab. There's always one less book than kids. Even the ones who can't read enjoy the tussle over them.

I begin my series of Pew Snarls. There are ingenious silent devices utilized by mothers in church to register disapproval. From the side and back, the snarls look like smiles. Only another mother knows that these sweet maternal smiles cloak messages ranging from "Don't look up into the choir loft again" to "Wait till we get in the car."

A few of mine and their translations:

Sharp sudden glance, mouth turned up means kneel or stand or do what the grownups are doing.

Long, hard look, mouth turned up means I dare you to do that again.

Naive, innocent glance with mouth turned up means surely no child of mine would behave like that on purpose.

Patient long-enduring look with mouth turned up means watch it!

13

Touch on shoulder with mouth up means quit shaking the pew.

And so on.

It continues during the sermon and continues and continues and continues . . .

The sermon ends. We go into the home stretch. Make it through Communion with only one or two rearrangements of children.

The Mass is ended. We go in relief. Resume normal behavior. Relax. Enjoy. Celebrate.

"Was I good?" they ask.

I nod magnanimously.

"*Now* can we go hiking today?"

We smile, "Yes, after breakfast we'll head for the mountains."

It's always nice to celebrate the Lord's Day.

VI
Can We Keep It, Mom?

They found a hamster in a cage in the local Goodwill box the other day, and there's been quite an uproar over it. I just can't share the tut-tuts of others toward some-one who would rid herself of an unwanted varmint in this way. I said to myself, "Now, there's a mother who'll go far." I have boundless admiration for her and I expect a few other mothers to share their admiration, secretly.

"But, Mom," asked one of mine, "how do you know it was a mother?"

Foolish Child. It takes one to know one. Who but a mother would assess the situation and solve the prob-lem so ingeniously? She is the one who accepts the pet with grave reservations in the first place. She is the one who hears fervent pledges, promises and vows that the children will feed, love, and clean up after the varmint. Likewise, she is the one who feeds, loves and cleans after the first week.

Mothers are not supposed to dislike pets. We read from the pet cult that a pet teaches children all kinds of responsibility and values. Well, that may be.

It teaches children that Mom can't stand by and watch a pet starve even if she doesn't like it. It teaches them that they don't have to keep their word, and that when Mom finally has enough, she will find a good

15

home for the displaced orphan. It teaches children, in short, that when the novelty wears off, Mom goes on.

So what does the average mother do when she starts getting petitis? She begins calling her friends to see if they'll take the hamster, gerbil, kitty, or canary off her hands. It's a matter of risking her friends to save her sanity.

But this mother, the Goodwill mother, showed a touch of genius. She didn't lose a friend; she just shared the joy of a pet with the less fortunate. Who can fault her? Those who are horrified at the idea that the poor little hamster might have gone airless for the two days before he was picked up aren't familiar with the lifestyle of hamsters, who enjoy disappearing and lurking in the bottom of the clothes hamper, giving the laundress a leg up on her coronary.

Those who worried that the little creature might have starved don't know that a hamster's favorite dish is newspaper to rip into thousands of tiny pieces, followed by socks to gnaw through. Goodwill depositories are long on grocery sacks containing castoff clothing, so it's a veritable feast for a rodent, which is the family of the hamster, after all.

Her solution was surely more humane than the man who put kitties in Trick Or Treat sacks a couple of years ago, and it's a lot better than turning the cage-born creatures loose on a strange farm to defend themselves against unfamiliar predators and weather.

As for me, I wish the woman would identify herself. I'll bet she's developed quite a few other techniques she could share with us. I wonder how she handles the before-school stomach aches that disappear around 10 A.M. Or the But-Mother-Everybody-Does-It routine. Or the lost library book trauma. Or the Casper-the-

Ghost syndrome: Nobody ate the cookies.

If we can have Nobel, Pulitzer, and Heisman awards, can we afford not to honor maternal showmanship? Let's face it, a woman who puts a hamster in the Goodwill box is never going to make Mother of the Year. But surely she has contributed something of value for the rest of us out here in kitchenland. Here's a thank-you, Nameless Mother, from a peer who isn't going to worry about pet disposal in the future.

VII
When I Was His Age . . .

For a subculture that detests hearing adults say, "When I was your age," children certainly make use of the technique with one another. One common complaint in the family room is the petulant wail of an older child who feels the younger one is being treated more generously than he was at that age.

It goes like this. "How come he gets to stay up till 8:30? When I was his age, I had to be in bed by 8."

Or, "Boy, she sure is lucky. I used to get spanked for doing that."

Or, "I didn't used to get paid for baby sitting when you just went to the library."

It's all executed with the proper look of accusation and injured tone that masks the unspoken *Therefore*: *therefore* you don't love me as much as you love him. Some children have it perfected to the degree that parents get panicky and rescind all rules, or make it up to the older one for being so cruel to him a few years back.

Other parents use other techniques to keep the complaint in perspective. One mother of eight handles it this way. When the child complains that she didn't get to go somewhere until she was in eighth grade whereas her younger sister gets to go in seventh grade, the mother says either "That's because you were such a fine example that she learned excellent behavior from you," or "When we saw how you turned out, we decided to change our rules." Either one is unanswerable by a whining sibling.

Another parent, this time a father, thoroughly tired of having to justify every rule in retrospect, responds simply, "That's because we like him better than you." After every child is told this a number of times, he knows it can't be true. He also knows his complaint isn't having the desired effect.

I use the Parable of the Vineyard technique. I've never particularly liked that parable. I don't think it was fair to pay all the workers the same, and I suspect that if Christ used it today, he'd have the social reformers on his back.

But it's a handy parable to have around when one child starts complaining about being mistreated. The first time I used it, one of our children had complained that he received less allowance at age seven than our present seven-year-old.

I offered the usual inflation explanation, but he didn't buy it. I tried a couple of other justifications which he also didn't accept. So I said, "Sit down. I want to tell you a parable . . ." and I related the Parable of the Vineyard.

He listened and said, "I don't think that was fair," and walked off. I didn't have to tell him I agreed and I didn't have to answer any more complaints about corrupting a seven-year-old by giving him a dime instead of a nickel.

A week later, another child complained that *he* never got to go to a real live stage play at age seven, so I said, "Let me tell you a parable." His reaction was similar.

A few weeks later, one of the eldest began complaining to another of the eldest in loud tones in front of us about our leniency with a younger child when the other cautioned, "Shh . . . we'll have to listen to that dumb parable again," and they tip-toed out.

You know, I'm beginning to like that parable.

VIII
A Miracle of Tongues

We took our youngest child to church with us when he was four—just Steve alone, without the other kids. And he discovered he could talk.

So did we. Steve started talking with the ignition and didn't stop until he bumped his jaw on the holy water font.

Poor youngest child. Prior to this time, others always interrupted him or, worse, finished his sentences for him so they could get on with the more important ideas in the world.

He'd been living in a world of, "Look at the—", and "Guess what I—?" and "Ya know what? I—". On the way to church his discovery of the complete sentence was a joy to witness. He blurted out, "Mom, can I—?" and automatically stopped.

"Can you what?" I asked.

"What what?" He was in shock. Normally, at this point, the poor kid regressed into himself. But not Sunday. He broke into a broad smile and said expansively, "Mom, can I get the song books at Mass today?"

Then he let the weight of the miracle resound. He had finished a statement. He had conquered communication. He had made an impact upon the airways. He was a bona fide listened-to-person.

"Sure you can, Steve," I replied, for once certain that

a second child wouldn't protest, "But it's my turn."

That was when Steve launched a line of conversation that was unbelievable only to anyone who hasn't been around a stifled four-year-old. What he said was immaterial. He had the uncontested floor and he used it like a seasoned sportscaster. As soon as his line of conversation began to weaken, he swung his head to the other car window, spotted something—anything—and began anew. It went something like this:

"Well, did you see those birds on those wires? Wonder what they had for breakfast. Fords have a birdhouse but Kirk only has a dune buggy . . . well, when I get big I'm gonna grow a beard but Grandpa doesn't ever have to water his lawn . . ."

Twenty minutes of this can get to anyone but the novelty of hearing his voice lulled us to listen as we rode sleepily toward church. It continued on the way home, unabated.

It was at brunch that the shoe fell. Steve's newfound verbal domain had traversed from novelty to right in just one morning, but the older kids weren't giving up that easily. When Steve began a rambling sentence, one of the others cut in with typical older-sibling arrogance, but this time Steve kept right on talking. The kids looked at him in wonder and then at us.

Weren't we going to stop him? We didn't get involved. Older children are always outraged when the youngest begins to stake out his territorial imperative. Besides, Steve was holding his own. His new bearing demanded a bit of respect.

"Wow!" said a daughter when Steve finally had to pause for a bite of donut. "What happened at church this morning?"

My husband, Steve, and I smiled at one another. "I guess you could call it the miracle of tongues," quipped my husband. And Steve sat proudly as the other children stared at him with new respect.

IX
Family Communication
Is . . . Well . . . You Know . . .

Sometimes I think we don't communicate in our family. We just guess. The last time anyone completed a sentence around here was Thanksgiving a few years ago when we asked the baby to show off his new verbal powers. We allowed him to say to his grandparents, "I like Sesame Street."

He actually said that: subject, verb and object in traditional order without being interrupted. He set a record for completing a sentence at the youngest age in our family.

Whenever anyone starts touting the necessity of family communication, I count his kids. When he says, "It's vital that parents allow their children to finish a sentence," I count his I.Q.

My children don't finish sentences, unless you count, "You know," as a clinching thought, as in:

". . . and then we'll, you know . . ."

or

"and the teacher said, you know . . ."

or

"I did it because, you know . . ."

If I ever waited for them to end their sentences, they

would be as uncomfortable as they are waiting for the spanking I promise and promptly forget.

We live in a fast world. Why wait for someone to finish a thought when we've already guessed it? Here's a typical conversation in our home:

3:30 p.m. Slam. "Hi, Mom, What's for—?"

"First you—"

"—okay."

"And hang—"

"—Okaaay."

"What about your library—"

"No panic. New cookies? How many?"

"Two. Early supper—"

"Yeah, game—"

Now *that* is communication at its purest. Maybe it's mystifying to an outsider, but to any mother and child it makes good sense. If the first question a child asks upon arriving home from school daily is, "What's for snack?" then why should he have to ask it at all? Why not, "Hi, Mom, what's for—?" She knows what he means.

Conversation is even more succinct between husband and wife. The timing is different. I usually think of the Important Issues at the end of a long day when our heads are on the pillows and we've said goodnight.

Silence strikes me. Can it really be quiet? "Oh, that reminds me," I say. "Did I tell you the Rocks have a new grandson?"

"Ummm," emanates from the neighboring pillow.

I am silent for a couple of minutes and then I recall, "By the way, the Ford is making funny noises in reverse."

"Ummmm," same noise, same pillow.

This intriguing exchange of ideas continues until I'm

answered with long sighs of slumber and I give up. How does one communicate with a bunch of feathers encircling a snore?

The family seems to me to be communicating very well, a bit too well to suit me. Once, just once, I'd like to be introduced all the way to the end: "Mom, this is Ginger. Ginger, this is my mom," instead of, "And this is—can we—oh, new strawberries—how many?"

We're communicating only too well, thank you. My son, what's-his-name, just said, you know . . .

X
How Parents Learn To Talk

We all know how children develop. We study their speech patterns to learn how old they are. At age two, for example, the child's chief word is, "Mine." No matter what a two-year-old grabs, be it his security blanket, his mother's hair or the cat, he hangs on fiercely and shouts, "Mine, Mine, Mine!" If he does this, we know he's a normal healthy two-year-old. If he doesn't, he has a normal healthy mother.

But what about a parent's development. In the plethora of books about children's speech patterns, I haven't discovered a single one on the development of a parent as shown by his speech. Yet, I hold that by listening in on a parent's daily chatter, we can discover, not his development, but the age of his children.

Here are my stages in a normal parent's speech pattern.

"Now, now, don't cry. The bottle will be ready in a minute."

"Smile for da-da. That's a good boy. Oooops, somebody bring a towel."

"Bye-bye. Wave bye-bye."

"Hello, doctor? His fever is up to 104 . . ."

"Num-num. Isn't this g-o-o-d?"

"No, no. Don't eat that. D-i-r-t-y."

"Upsy-daisy. Here, Mommy will kiss that owie."

"Don't touch that. No! No!"

"This is the last time I'm going to say that."

"Hello, doctor? He's still bleeding a little."

"Good boy. Big boy. We'll tell Daddy about that when he gets home."

"Say hello to Aunt Mae on the phone—no, this end."

"Pick it up."

"Put it down."

"Because big boys don't do that."

"Hello, doctor? This time it's his foot . . ."

"Eat it or no dessert."

"Because I said so."

"I already answered that."

"Hello, Emergency Room?"

"Here's your milk money."

"Ask your father."

"He did! Wait till his father gets home."

"I don't care what the other kids get to do."

"No TV until your math improves."

"Look at this room!"

"HELLO, is this the orthodontist's office?"

"Oh, motherrrr yourself."

"Whadya mean, yuck?"

"Get off the phone."

"You're grounded until your math improves."

"No, you can't go out with that bunch."

"We aren't voting on it."

"Why don't you get your hair cut?"

"Turn down that music."

"Who ate our supper?"

"We'll see."

"No, we need you to babysit for us tonight."

"Remember, it's the only car we have."

"Yes, officer, we understand."

"Get off the phone."

"No scholarship, no college."

"Write us every week."

"No more checks until your math improves."

"We're so proud of our graduate."

"She's lovely, son. Have you set a date?"

"You are? When? Call us as soon as it's born."

"Now, now. The bottle will be ready in a minute. Grandma's hurrying."

XI
Because I Said So

It was at a lecture on parenting that I heard it, so help me God. The noted psychologist summed up a detailed list of what really bugs kids with the ultimate parental sin: answering the child with, "Because I said so."

Feeling a bit nervous, I sent some sidelong glances at the parents seated around me, only to find them telegraphing their nervousness back. However, few of us were ready for that psychologist's ultimate statement: "Quite frankly, I can't think of any situation that justifies a parent in saying to a child, 'Because I said so.' "

Well, Doctor, I can. As a fer-instance, let's take a typical 4:35 P.M. family situation. Mom is behind the wheel, having picked up one child from CCD and another from the allergist, and is on the way to nab a third from the bus stop in front of which the child has promised to be standing.

Predictably, no child. Mom stops in the rush hour No Stopping lane, turns to the CCD child and says, "Quick! Run into the drugstore and get Benny while I pretend the car has stalled."

The child eyes her balefully. "I went last time. How come I have to go instead of Jean-Anne?"

Now, according to the psychologist, Mom will patiently explore alternatives, gently and rationally leading the child to maturity by discussing what a family is and how one becomes a contributing member thereof. However, according to reality, Mom, voice edged in hysteria, will shout, "BECAUSE I SAID SO!"

Wrong it may be, but effective, considering the state of traffic today.

A second occasion calling for "Because I said so" is when the child is bored and doesn't really want an answer but a kitchen talk show:

"Can I spend tonight at Jerry's?"

"Not tonight. You've invited Timmy over."

"Why can't we both go over to Jerry's?"

"Because it isn't polite to invite someone here and then go to someone else's home. Besides, Timmy's mom might not like it."

"Why can't you call her?"

"Because there's no reason to. Timmy is your guest here tonight."

"But why can't we go to Jerry's?"

"BECAUSE I SAID SO!"

A third occasion results when the parent has given ten perfectly good reasons but the child has rejected them all, finally forcing the parent to the unreasonable response.

"Wear your heavy coat, Melissa."

"How come?"

"It's 34 degrees and snowing."

"But it's March. Why do I have to wear it in March?"

"Because you just got over bronchitis."

"I'm not coughing any more. Why do I have to wear it when I'm not coughing?"

Well, you get the idea. It's only a matter of words to, "BECAUSE I SAID SO!" Meanwhile the child smirks, getting the reaction she wanted, all the while buttoning on her heavy coat.

Admittedly, nobody likes to hear "Because I said so." Oh, it's called different things out in society: Company Policy, School Regulations, and Church Law. But whatever it's called, it comes back to, "Because I said so" because . . . ultimately . . . somebody's got to say so.

XII
Give Me That Old
Fifties Wardrobe

I used to wonder what made certain mothers popular with other teenagers. For a long time I thought it was because they were more understanding, then more fun, finally more relevant. I couldn't have been more wrong.

The most popular mothers in our town are the ones who saved their fifties clothes. Since the advent of *American Graffiti*, *Happy Days*, and the Fonz, every high school worth its decibels holds an annual fifties sock hop to which the kids flock looking like the cast from American Bandstand.

The boys don't have a problem. They can usually find some baggy pants stashed away among the fishing gear and enough Vaseline to slick their longish hair back into a reasonable duck tail. All they need to complete their Look is an old-fashioned letter sweater and that's something dads never throw away. They may throw away their white oxfords because they're going out of style or their wide ties just as they're coming back into style but they'll never, repeat, never throw away a letter sweater.

But the girls do have a problem. Sure, they can hitch their long locks into a high curly pony tail and find someone with a pair of today's saddle shoes. But they need the bulky sweaters and pleated skirts of distant memory in these days of soft knits and wrap-around skirts. And to be the real hit of the ball, they need to find one of those super relics of the early fifties, a long black ballerina skirt decorated with a poodle. We all had them.

Alas, few mothers saved such garb. Foolishly we dumped them into St. Vincent bags when permanent press and maternity tops became more our style. I've found that's no excuse.

"But, Mom, why didn't you save at least one fifties skirt?"

"Because they didn't fit me in the sixties."

"But they would fit *me* now."

"Forgive me," I reply. "To make you feel better, I saved my maternity tops for you."

"Gross."

In an attempt to offset such parental negligence, I suggest a call to Mrs. Save Everything down the block.

"No, somebody already called her," I hear. "The only mothers with the neat fifties clothes are Mrs. Hanson, Abernathy, and Custer. I'm third in line for Mrs. Custer's skirt if the other two don't get dates. Or . . ." Pause, "I'm hoping they'll get sick . . ." A quick look at me, "But not too sick."

It's terrible to be a parent failure, particularly when a girl's social future depends on a poodle skirt.

Come to think of it, I did save that poodle skirt. I cut it up to make a Frankenstein cape ten Halloweens ago. After that it became a pirate flag and then I lost track of it.

But I'm not going to fail my daughter again. I'm saving all her seventies clothes for her daughter 25 years from now. Yup, both pairs.

34

XIII
Our Sanity Corner

"Set aside a table in a corner where the children can dabble to their hearts' content," emphasized the prominent art consultant in an article. Like any good middle-class mother who feels intimidated if she doesn't furnish cultural advantages to develop her children's talents, I scurried about setting up a family Art Table.

My biggest difficulty was in finding a corner unoccupied by baby furniture or old magazines. Finally, I moved an old rocking horse, evacuated the spiders, and doled out the dust balls to outstretched hands eager to get on with an original game called "Who Can Blow Them Farthest?"

After covering our second-best card table with layers of plastic sheeting, terry cloth, and newspapers, I stocked our Art Corner. Some twelve dollars later, I surveyed my attempt with maternal satisfaction. Ten half-inch brushes made for little hands, heavy water containers, tempera paint blocks in a dozen shades, real art paper, a roll of heavy butcher paper for murals, and sundry items like sponges and colored chalk completed the inventory.

Then I called in my eager artists, plus a couple of friends who had kept up with my progress. "Create," I smiled, and left them to their inspiration as I wound my way to the ironing board to finish a most uncreative basket of wrinkled shirts and jeans.

Create they did. Within an hour, I had enough art work to cover four refrigerators—and they showed no signs of letup. I had to pry them away for lunch where, when I left the room to put paint-stained shirts and jeans in the washer, I overheard them discussing which color paint tasted better. Under cross-examination—and I mean cross—they insisted that any tasting was purely accidental. "When we put the brush handles in our mouths to keep the other kids from getting them, we sometimes get a taste of paint, that's all," explained the one who shows signs of becoming a successful lawyer some day.

We then had a dual lesson on sharing and on not eating the paint. Not only was it unhealthy, I pointed out, but also expensive. By the time their father came home from work, the art paper was depleted and I was elated. Not only had they found a creative outlet, but they hadn't asked once all day long, "What can we do?" Even more optimistic was the fact that they forgot to watch Carnage Cartoons and The Planets Collide, our two concessions to their non-cultural television development.

Short-Lived. However, we faced a real problem— what to do with the art masterpieces. I suggested that each child choose ten to display at home and inundate the relatives and neighbors with the rest. They agreed eagerly and spent the evening delivering original art works to neighbors (from whose kids I will eventually buy Kool-Aid and Easter Seals in return). Excitedly, I related to my husband how this was The Answer. It was going to be a short summer after all, I rejoiced. I ran to the store for more art supplies as he dutifully praised a few dozen paintings, one at a time.

36

My exultation was unbounded—and short-lived. Hardly had I swung out of bed the following morning when I was assailed with, "What can we do?" in several pitches.

"Why, what about the Art Corner?" I responded cheerfully.

"Oh, we did that already. We don't want to paint anymore."

And they didn't. Except under duress, they haven't gone near the well-stocked and dusty Art Corner since. The paints dried up, the paper turned yellow, and the spiders came home to spin. Occasionally, I think that maybe that one glorious and creative day was worth it; but then I realize that, for that price, we could have taken the family to the mountains for an equally glorious and creative day. Still, I can't bring myself to dismantle that symbol of culture. I keep hoping that some rainy day, a future Van Gogh, a late bloomer, might be drawn by the seclusion and supplies to create once again.

Science Corner. My husband didn't mention the unused Art Corner until the Science Corner came into being. "Set aside a table in a corner where the children can experiment, display their discoveries of nature, and store their specimens," said the elementary science supervisor. Undaunted, I decided to furnish a Science Corner, but when I looked around I discovered our supply of corners was diminishing fast. Outgrown tricycles, baby bed rails, and old draperies destined to become theatrical costumes consumed all available space. "Why not use the Art Corner?" suggested my husband.

His idea just intensified my futile search. I ended up moving my ironing gear into the middle of the room to furnish space for a Science Corner. Unfortunately, the

Science Corner has had a much longer life span than the Art Corner. I haven't been able to kill it yet. I didn't know what we were inviting when we encouraged the kids to collect anything that crawled, flew, multiplied, or escaped.

One of our first purchases, as suggested by the science supervisor, was a butterfly net. It has been invaluable, not for finding insects originally, but for recovering them around the house. Somehow, the kids seem able to capture anything that moves in the great outer world without any difficulty, but let the same creature get out of his cage or bottle in the house and he will defy capture in an eight by eight room.

At last count we have recovered, somewhere in our home, sixteen rolypolys, a couple dozen grasshoppers, several butterflies, a bumble bee, two feet of caterpillars, and untold numbers of ladybugs, spiders, and less definable species. Presently, we have at large a frog, an angleworm, and "something black with eyes," as reported to me at breakfast by a five-year-old. This leaves only to our imagination the hordes that must have escaped without our notice.

It can be nerve-wracking when there's an escape. If I've been forewarned that a crawling science project is on the loose, I "see" it a dozen times in the form of a bread crust, a bacon bit, or a crayon before it emerges as a reality. One day I looked down in time to stop a young one from putting a curled up roly-poly in the pepper grinder because it so closely resembled a peppercorn. Probably most traumatic was the time I overheard one son say to another, "Don't tell Mom it got away. She'll be scared." That was several months ago and I'm still watching warily for "it"—whatever it might be.

Another time, on a snowy November evening, some startled guests watched an elusive late October grasshopper hop from the corner fringe on our living room rug. Without interrupting himself, my husband casually reached out for the butterfly net, captured the hopper, and called one of his keepers to return him to the Science Table. There was no comment but a noticeable sigh of relief when it was gone.

In addition to insects and small animals, we have a good supply of rocks, weeds, pine cones, and the like which can be transported into our home legally under the guise of science. I discouraged the algae and put my foot down on the decayed log with grubs, but for the most part the Science Corner can be said to be the most active corner in the house. Oh, yes, I did persuade my husband to smuggle the horned toad out one dark night. I couldn't stand those blinking eyes staring at me as I ironed. Other than that, I encouraged the science culture.

Music Corner. The Music Corner was a different story. Maybe it was because we became dependent on corners by this time or that we just wanted to get all those noisy instruments in one spot, but the Music Corner can't be blamed on any expert. It was our idea entirely. It began when a bachelor uncle gave each of our kids a drum for Christmas. Shortly thereafter, they collected a guitar, some xylophones, fifes, and the like.

In desperation, I cleaned out the corner next to the piano and stated firmly that, from then on, anytime anyone wanted to make music it was to be in that corner. That was a glorious goof. Nothing encourages noise like noise, and the Music Corner furnished far more noise than music. Unfortunately, it, too, remains a popular spot.

Sanity Corner. Last week, my husband and I were trying to discuss something in the vicinity of the Corners. When a child sauntered over to the Music Corner and began absently drumming on the piano, we raised our voices a little. Then a few more joined in and we raised our voices a lot. Suddenly, an enraged shout came from the Science Corner. "Who broke into the cocoon?" Charges and denials flew hotly about as we tried to restore tranquility.

Finally, we conceded defeat and headed for the farthest room in the house, our bedroom. That is how our Sanity Corner was born. In mute agreement, we moved out a hamper, a cedar chest, and a dressing table. We moved in two easy chairs, footstools, a magazine rack, and some lamps. Our children watched us in uneasy silence, impressed with our determination.

Then my husband explained that silence and serenity are both educational and cultural and that this one corner was to remain ours. Any child, musical instrument, or eight-legged pet which strayed near it would be destroyed, he emphasized. Harsh words, but we haven't been disturbed.

The Science and Music Corners live on, active and noisy, but we don't care. We've proved that we can have our culture and sanity, too.

XIV
What Does Your Husband Do?

Ever since I was in college and asked by a sorority rush girl, "What does your father do?" I've sabotaged that question. It's a subtle way of asking, "Where do you stand on the economic ladder?" or "Just how important are you socially?"

People who wouldn't consider asking the blunt question, "How much do you make?" or "What are you worth?" will smile after an introduction, make a pleasantry or two and get to the important question, "What does your husband do?"

Friends in government tell me it's even more blatant at cocktail parties where Washington wives introduce themselves and ask immediately, "What's your husband's GS?" If the rating isn't high enough, the wife drifts away to another spouse in an obvious case of, "Is your husband important enough for me to spend my time cultivating a friendship with you?"

The problem is simplified whenever there are titles: major, colonel, doctor, dean, monsignor, mayor, senator and judge. Some women are eager to divulge the rank or prestige of their husbands and sons, a situation ready-made for jokes, i.e., the Jewish mother running down the beach shouting, "Help! My son, the rabbi, is drowning!"

But the reality isn't fiction. It's an amusing pastime

among women to see how long it will take a wife whose own value is assessed through her husband's status to reveal it to a stranger. Some wives become very skilled in the art of rank-dropping.

I enjoy the reverse—subverting the question and frustrating the questioner. Unless the person has a right to know or the conversation naturally drifts into occupations, I figure it is rude to indulge in, "Pleased to meet you. Awfully hot, isn't it? What does your husband do, Mrs. Curran?"

So . . . I have several stock responses, the most usable being a smile and, "Oh, just about the same things other husbands do." That stops the first level of prestige-placers, but more determined ones come back with, "Oh, no," small laugh, "I mean what field is he in?"

"Field?" I ask quizzically.

At this, the interrogator is beginning to suspect she is being put on and she asks outright, "I mean where does he work?"

"Oh!" my turn to small-laugh, "at the corner of Ruger and First."

Even the most accomplished investigator has to give up at this. Other answers to, "What does your husband do?" are "He's in automobiles" (aren't we all?); "He nurses his ulcers" (prestigious); "He travels"; and "I wish I could tell you but I've never been able to figure it out myself." And then there's always the stricken look accompanied with, "I'd rather not talk about it."

If a man cuts to the quick with, "What does your husband do?" I cut back with, "What does your wife do?" I'm not judging his value by his wife's occupation and I'm not about to be judged by my husband's. I figure that the very least he could do is ask me first, "What do you do?" His initial question about my husband reveals to me that a woman's value lies through her husband's status and I don't accept that.

By now, I suppose you're all wondering what my husband does. But I don't mind telling *you*. He's in books.

XV
If It's Baby Jesus' Birthday, Where's His Cake?

Several Christmases ago I suffered much unnecessary anguish. As a Catholic mother of preschoolers, I tried to instill the meaning and joy of the holy season through such devices as making an Advent wreath, telling stories and teaching the joyful carols.

Apparently I was successful because the kids, both mine and the neighborhood's, immediately brought it down to their level, taking the parts of Mary and Joseph in their imaginative play and ad-libbing what can only be described as non-religious and homely dialogue.

I cringed each time I heard a little lisper replace a hallowed phrase with toddler vernacular: "Hiya, Mary. Isn't supper ready yet?" Finally, though, the Holy Spirit struck me and I realized that the young ones were making the simple and compelling Christmas story meaningful by bringing it down to their own terms. They intended no irreverence—I was the one that was reading it in.

When I relaxed and began to enjoy their enactment of the story through innocent eyes, I realized how much we adults cloud the thrilling tale by using reverential but unintelligible phraseology and atmosphere.

A few days after I had related the Christmas story the

first time, I was startled to see the band of preschoolers marching around the basement, to the tune of "Mulberry Bush," singing, "This is the way we follow the star, follow the star, follow the star . . ."

Intrigued, I split my attention between them and my ironing, and ended up seeing the Christmas story as it appears to three- and four-year-olds. The star-followers knocked at the den door and a young girl holding a teddy bear opened it, saying, "Why, hello, three kings. I'm Mary. Won't you come in and have a cup of coffee?"

In the days that followed, I realized how much of the Christmas tale they were absorbing by keeping one ear tuned in on their play. Each day, of course, the story changed to fit their needs or moods. If there were many children, the three kings became four or five. Once Jesus was twins. If the flu kept a few kids home, Mary and Joseph complained about those slow kings, who never did make it.

One day I heard the three kings offer their gifts to Mary.

"Here's some money for Jesus," said one.

"Thank you. I'll put it in His bank," said Mary.

"No, no," said this king, no spoil-sport he. "It's for Him to spend at the dime store."

Another king entered, "I've got some incense for Him."

"What's incense?" asked Mary.

"Oh," replied the young king (who had obviously done some research on the question), "it's some good-smelling smoke . . . sort of like bacon smoke."

It didn't seem to bother the young ones to rewrite history: One day the innkeeper didn't turn Mary and Joseph down, and the turn of events didn't disrupt the actors' aplomb at all. However, when the same switch occurred the next day, the young Joseph said loudly, "Now, look, you guys. Jesus has to be born in a manger, because Mary rode on a donkey and the three kings rode on their camels and the shepherds rode on their sheep and they *had* to have a barn for all those animals."

That Mary wasn't encumbered by modern conveniences didn't stop their appearance in the play. Once, in the manger, when the phone rang, Joseph said, "Mary, it's an angel."

"What does she want?"

"I don't know . . . all she says is 'gloria.' "

Individual home habits got an airing, too, and my ears burned the day I heard my daughter, playing Mary, say sternly, "Jesus, if You don't hush, I'll have Joseph get the ruler."

It made me feel better the next day to hear a little neighborhood Mary say, "Well, Jesus, we'd better hurry and start supper before Joseph gets home or he'll wonder what we've been doing all day."

Another time, a visiting shepherd asked Mary why she had no Christmas tree in the manger. She replied casually, "Oh, Joseph has just been too lazy to put it up."

Sometimes I became a little concerned about the arguments over the daily parts. No one wanted to be Jesus because He couldn't talk, so they usually ended up using a doll or stuffed toy. Everyone wanted to be Mary or Joseph, so they had to take turns.

One day I heard a defiant voice ring up from the basement, "Now, I'm going to be Joseph and you're a king—and you have to wait for that other king to get his snow-pants and boots off."

The youngsters didn't seem to mind mixing the Christmas story in with modern commercial symbols, and it wasn't at all unusual to have Rudolph sitting in the manger alongside the camels. One day a bored actor playing Jesus sang out from His cradle (an upside-down card table), "Oh, bring me a figgy pudding . . . and bring it right now."

"Just a minute," answered Mary. "I'm warming it up."

I never did get them straightened out on the misunderstanding arising from the words in "Away in a Manger." Some of them insisted that a person representing God should stand by the cradle because of the verse: ". . . and the little Lord Jesus look down from the sky and stay by my cradle till morning is night." While I was trying to explain that that last word was nigh, not night, they were dividing into factions over whether someone should stand next to the cradle. I left the scene of the argument, which soon resolved itself by the number of kids available. It was a good part for the youngest child if he wasn't needed elsewhere.

Frankly, the Christmas story was getting out of hand, and I was happy to see the day approaching so they could lose themselves in other new-year imaginative play. My sense of propriety had been razed enough, however, to enjoy their bringing the story to life on their hero level. After all, if they were idolizing Mary Poppins, Batman, and the like, surely there was room for Jesus.

But I had no idea how long they retained the facets of Christmas. One day in late spring, when my four-year-old daughter asked me if we could ever get another baby, I replied, "Maybe if we pray very hard, God will send us one."

She replied most earnestly, "Why don't we just get another Advent wreath?"

I realized then that she had confused the symbolism

with the story and I decided against trying to explain it further at the time. And I'm still undecided on whether or not we should get one this year. I'll wait and see how much nerve I have.

XVI
I Wonder Why
We Weren't Invited

The aroma of Christmas cookies baking drew the kindergarten crowd away from the pages of the toy catalogue and into my kitchen momentarily. Five-year-old Rob, mastering the feat of eating through a stack of four cookies simultaneously, decided to engage me in crumb-impeded conversation: "Hey, are ya goin' to the party down the block tonight?"

I murmured an appropriate adult noise without answering his question. Not to be shut off, he added, "My mom and dad are goin'. Boy, it's goin' to be a neat party. My mom had her hair done."

Too busy to rise to the bait, I smiled vaguely in his direction. Disappointed at my lack of response, Rob said as he sauntered off, "Anyway, I wonder why you weren't invited."

My head jerked up. Why wasn't I invited? Did he know more than he was wondering?

I didn't care about the party, or who was hosting it, or who was going to it. After a few yuletide evenings of girdle and hors d'oeuvres, I didn't mind staying home. No, I didn't care about not being invited, but I *did* care about having the neighborhood juveniles wonder why I wasn't invited.

I never discovered why I wasn't invited, or who was having the party, for that matter. After I finished the cookies and ho-ho'd my way through four sets of entangled tree lights, I was too tired even to peek out the front window. But why is it that two years later, I can't even remember where Rob moved or what he looked like, but I can recall his remark instantly?

Every Christmas I learn all over again that 'tis not only the season to be jolly but also evasive. From about December 10 on, a different set of social rules takes precedence. Any other time of the year, for example, you can mention to a friend at the supermarket that you are tired because you stayed out too late the night before.

But if you make that mistake during eggnog season, a questioning look enters her eyes and you can almost hear her suspicious mind asking: Where was she? Who had the party? Why wasn't I invited?

There are many problems involved in entertaining during the sensitive season. Overflowing guest lists often force hosts to scratch friends' names unmercifully. "By the time I invite all those I owe invitations to, I don't have room for the ones I like," is a common complaint among hostesses. It also causes a most unlikely gathering of guests. One couple pared their list to the bone and then sat down to analyze it. The discussion went like this:

"We can't have the Olsons and the Roberts, too. They're both angling for the same job. And we'd better skip either the Axels or the Hintons since they had that fight over their kids' fight."

They continued on like that until they had a totally harmonious but utterly boring group. Then, some of their favorite uninvited friends heard about the party and scratched the hosts off their future guest list.

Another couple played musical guests with a list until they were certain they had no conflicts in personality. But their plans went awry when a tag-along guest turned out to be the former wife of a guest husband.

"We didn't know what to do because she still had his last name, so we just introduced her by her first name," the hostess told me. "The former husband didn't mind but his wife ripped down all the mistletoe in the house. I still get the hives just thinking about that party."

Another phenomenon of this busy party season is that of inscrutability. If you have been at the same party the previous evening with some of the other guests, none of you must give any indication of it or the omitted guests will wonder who left them out. This can lead to some pretty awkward buffet conversations. Many's the wife who's had to spike-heel her husband as he launched into a conversation with: "I was thinking about what you said last night . . ." or "Boy, that guy had some weird ideas about taxes, didn't he?"

There's the embarrassment, too, of two friends issuing invitations for the same evening, using nearly identical guest lists. It usually resolves itself in the holiday spirit if each one has sent an invitation to the other. But it's rough on the one who left the other hostess out. One woman, finding herself in that dilemma, wrote out a quick invitation and ran over to sneak it into her friend's mailbox. She was almost successful. The family's three-year-old caught her with her hand in the mailbox. "We don't go in that way," he lisped nonchalantly. "We go in the door."

What usually happens is that both hostesses omit each other and are unknowingly competing for the same guests. The guests, forced to choose between the two, try to wedge both parties in.

We had the uncomfortable experience of "crossing"

parties last year and bumping into guests doing the same thing. We left the Smith party a little early to stop in at the Jones party. Just as we arrived, some friends were leaving to drop in at the Smiths. Eventually all those we had already said goodbye to at our first party ended up at the second.

The one thing we can't count on is children. They believe us when we tell them it's wrong to lie, so they tell on us. If we're off to a party at the Hansens and our good friends, the Woods, telephone, they're not only going to hear about our destination but are apt to be treated to a full description of what we wore and who is babysitting. They may even close the phone conversation with, "I wonder why you weren't invited," for all we know.

Of course, it works to our advantage, too. One four-year-old from up the block spent a whole afternoon "helping" me decorate the tree and enlivened the occasion with this type of monologue:

". . . and Daddy said we couldn't invite the Harolds 'cause he drinks too much and Mommy said so do you so we're inviting the Harolds as long as we have to invite the Wrights because she babysits us for free. And we're invitin' you because we like you and your daddy even if your dog barks a lot. We wanted to invite the Browns but they wouldn't fit and we aren't invitin' the Homers 'cause they didn't invite us."

But now it's time for another season of adult duplicity. I wonder if we wouldn't be much better off spreading the gaiety throughout the year and saving the wear and tear on the conscience. I wonder if we'll be able to cut down our guest list without losing any friends this year. I wonder where George Anderson was going last year when he said goodbye at the party with, "See you all tomorrow night." I wonder why I wasn't invited . . .

52

XVII
But It's Not Cold Out

I watched Carter's inaugural festivities along with the rest of the country and, like so many others, I was impressed with the pomp and ceremony involved.

But what really impressed me had nothing to do with speeches, power, or promises. The great moment for me was when the Carters, ready to embark upon their inaugural walk, had to stop first to button Amy's coat. I nearly came out of the dishwater. "They're real people," I shouted to the cat. "Their daughter doesn't button her coat in sub-zero weather, either."

It was a moment to savor. Minutes after President Carter quoted Micah on remaining humble, he had the opportunity to show millions of parents that Presidential power, as formidable as it is in regulating hot and cold wars, has no effect whatsoever on hot and cold children.

I've lost the battle with my children. It's an axiom of Curran household law that it's never cold outside. Never mind that there are severe storm warnings. Ignore the thermometer calling for help outside the window. Pay no attention that the mailman is just a pair of eyes and a puff of steam emanating out of a knitted mask. "It's not cold out, Mom."

I used to think it was something they would outgrow, that when they got a little bigger they'd feel a little colder, but I was wrong. As they grow past me, I find myself reaching up to fasten buttons or tie a hood.

The hood. Oh, I should never have mentioned it. Children don't seem to have a very good idea of why it's there. Some use it to hang up the coat, others chew on the tie. Usually it becomes part of snow games—trying to stuff snowballs into another's hood and then slapping it on his head. Most often, it just lies there, as children come in from school with scarlet ears and frosted hair.

I used to ask, "Why didn't you wear your hood?" but the answers unnerved me. "What hood?" "I can't see with it on," and the inevitable, "It isn't cold outside."

My teenager has her own axiom to grind: "When Mom is cold, we've got to put on coats." Well, she has a point, I admit, but usually as Mom goes so goes the rest of the world. Blaming me for chills isn't fair when the temperature is ten degrees. There have been a few times I've relented to their before-school pleas of, "Please, can't we wear our sweaters today? It's broiling out there," and watched the wind chill factor climb so alarmingly by 10 A.M. that I drove to school with their warm coats only to humiliate them by being. "Why'd ya bring this?" they ask, ears red from having their mother appear in the hallway or on the playground.

I recall with embarrassment driving home one afternoon and seeing a little boy sledding in just a sweatshirt and jeans. "What kind of mother would let her child . . ." I began, and then recognized one of my Very Own. Now I know what kind of mother . . . an old mother, a tired mother, a mother of hot children.

I doubt if the Carters planned that inaugural gesture, but if I were President, I'd keep on buttoning Amy. Of all the campaign buttons, these were the most endearing.

XVIII
A Handy Multiple Choice Test on Fathers

1. You can tell he's a father if: A) there's an odor of model airplane glue about him; B) grass clippings dribble out of his cuffs; C) he asks for two more free balloons at the service station; D) he takes an early plane home instead of spending another day at his convention in some exotic area.

2. The father is to the child as: A) the trunk is to the treehouse; B) the stick is to the popsicle; C) the refrigerator is to the teenager; D) the car is to the learner's permit. ~

3. Fathers are best described as: A) friends; B) fixers; C) giants; D) invincible; E) protectors; F) just dads.

4. Fathers were put on this earth to: A) build Pinewood Derby racers for Cub Scouts; B) be around when dark comes and things go bump in the night; C) save children from mothers; D) save mothers from children; E) eat daughter's first brownies and smile.

5. You can tell there's a dad in the house if: A) the car is parked straight in the garage; B) the shirts look like they're climbing into the hamper; C) there aren't any balls on the roof; D) the ice maker works.

6. You can tell dad is out of town when: A) the family eats dinner at the pancake house; B) all the lights on the

estate burn at night; C) Mom gets a helpless look when the car hums a new tune; D) the eldest son assumes a manly air as he takes the trash cans out.

7. The best fathers: A) like to take their sons and the BB gun and go to the mountains; B) like to take their daughters out to dinner; C) like to change babies; D) like mothers.

8. Dads are scariest when: A) they haven't shaved by Saturday noon; B) they give you That Look in church; C) it's icy and they aren't home from work when they should be; D) you think of what it would be like without them.

9. I think the reason we have fathers is: A) so we can have grandfathers; B) so we know what God looks like; C) so mom will have someone to have you ask when she doesn't want to say no; D) so we can have an allowance, a vacation, and a house.

10. Life without dads would be like: A) pro-football without TV; B) sickness without mom; C) corn on the cob without teeth; D) awful.

Results: All answers are correct.

XIX
A Cookbook of Mothers

I am grateful to some wonderful fourth graders for this chapter. I hope you enjoy it as much as I did reading their recipes and other motherabilia.

* * * * *

Recipe for a Good Mother
Take one mother and mix her up with five children, one dad, a dog and a gerbil. Add lots of food and take out all yelling. Bake this all together in a home for 50 years.

* * * * *

Recipe for a Grandma
   1 head of white hair
   2 kind-of-wrinkled hands
   1 big lap
   1 enormous house
   20 cookies

* * * * *

"I don't know why all other mothers look the same but mine is different. I mean when somebody else's mother comes into the class she just looks like an ordinary mother. Mine looks different, that's all."

Happy Family Stew
　Take one house.
　Add one mom and one dad.
　Mix with kids and dirt.
　Stir in a lot of love and tears.
　Season well with smiles.
　Let simmer for a lifetime.

* * * * *

How To Make a Grandma
　Grandmas don't have children. Instead they have grandchildren. Alot. Grandmas live in Iowa or Pencilvania and youshlly live with grandpas but not always. They always send two dollars for your birthday and more for your First Communion.

* * * * *

Recipe for a Terrific Mother
　She's got a soft voice. She likes pets. (Even tho she's alurgick to them) She's funny and tells good stories. She loves us but doesn't kiss us all the time. I think she would win the pilsberry bake-off contest for good mothers.

* * * * *

Moms
　Moms are people but not like other people. I mean they get mad and stuff but it doesn't scare you like when teachers do. Moms listen to you and make you feel better. Moms work in two places. At the office and at home. My mom is a very important person in her office and some day she might be boss. I am proud of my mom but I don't tell her I am. I don't know why.

XX
Mothers and Daughters

One year, I was asked to address a mother-daughter brunch and, since my daughter was invited, I asked her if she would like to speak on behalf of the daughters. She agreed and together we worked out the following definitions.

I wrote the definition as the mother sees it and Sarah read it and did the followup as the daughter sees it. It was a lot of fun and I offer it to you mothers to try with your children.

A *daughter* is someone who eats peanut butter on her toast for breakfast, peanut butter and jelly sandwiches for lunch, and then, when she goes to a restaurant for dinner, she asks, "Do you have anything with peanut butter here?"

A *mother* is someone who eats diet food all day so she can eat popcorn and pie all night.

A *daughter* is someone who combs and combs her hair and when it is just perfect she goes outside and hangs upside down from the trapeze.

A *mother* is someone who goes to the beauty shop to have her hair frosted so the grey won't show.

A *daughter* is someone who says, "Oh, mother," when she really means, "How dumb."

A *mother* is someone who says, "We'll see," when she means, "No."

A daughter is someone whose room is a disaster area, who's two weeks behind in piano practicing, and who says, "There's nothing to do."

A mother is someone whose desk is a disaster area, who's two weeks behind in her ironing, and who says, "Sure, we'll be glad to do it."

A daughter is someone who pretends to hate brothers, frogs and horror movies but really loves them.

A mother is someone who pretends to hate whiskers, chocolate candy and giggly girls but really loves them.

A daughter is someone who writes urgent notes like, "Mom, don't let me forget to take my library book tomorrow. Don't forget!!!!" And then she forgets to put the note on her mother's pillow.

A mother is someone who puts a thermometer in your mouth, tells you not to talk and then forgets about it for 45 minutes.

A daughter is someone who brings her mother hems to be lowered, tears to be kissed away, and hours of unforgettable joy.

A mother is someone who brings her daughter dishes to be washed, worries to be laughed away, and hours of unforgettable joy.

XXI
Mothers and Sons

I had a father, four brothers and a husband and I still wasn't prepared for a ten-year-old boy's view of school, church, and work. For a while I blamed it on his near-sightedness. Then he got glasses and nothing changed, except frequent trips to the optometrist to straighten out bent frames and replace cracked lenses.

Then I blamed it on his tonsils but all his tonsillec-tomy proved was that he could eat more. He still hated school, church, and work.

When I asked him, in exasperation, one day, "Well, just what is it you do like to do?" he pondered the question seriously and came up with, "I like to eat, to play and to watch television." Ask an honest question, you get an honest answer.

I understand this situation is peculiar to parents who have girls first. Girls like school. They rush home ex-citedly with a "project" and have it done before the boys remember whom they threw their project paper at. Boys recall their projects a half hour before school on deadline day, and instead of the lovely seed collections their sisters execute, they draw a quick picture of a flower on the back of a ripped-off calendar and label the parts, "leevs, petls, and routs."

Girls come rushing home from school, eager to spill daily academic tidbits like who likes who today and who has to pay 35 cents for wasting the gerbil food by pouring it in a friend's milk.

Boys don't come rushing home for anything but dinner. They wander home from school. Sometimes they shuffle, sometimes they loiter. Always they trespass. Sometimes it takes a boy fifteen minutes to cover half a block. This usually happens on the day he has an urgent appointment somewhere and his mother is sitting in the station wagon with the engine and her temper warmed up.

Girls tell all that's real or fancied about their teachers: "Mrs. Harrow drives an orange car with a Little League sticker on it. We think she might be a Little League coach because she has big feet. She's probably the only woman coach in the Little League and probably all the dads don't like her, ya know?"

Boys don't remember their teachers' names.

Girls stew for days over what they're going to wear for the school program. Boys tell their mothers the morning of the program that they have to have clean hands and a red and white striped sport coat.

Girls can discuss for hours which classes and subjects they like best. Boys like only three: recess, lunch and gym. The rest of the day is considered a waiting period.

Girls can't wait for Monday, boys can't wait for Friday. Girls can't wait for September, boys can't wait for June. Girls can't wait for the honor roll. Boys think it's some kind of bread.

And pity the parents of first girl-children when they start assigning chores to boy-children. Girls don't relish chores but they do them. Boys hate them and have to be dragged to them. Boys don't like doing men's work like emptying wastebaskets. They like doing boy's work like flying model airplanes and digging holes to trap horned toads.

Girls have the decency to pretend to like church and church school, even if they don't. Boys say outright, "I hate church." When parents patiently explain to boys why they should like going to church, boys nod and say, "Okay," and "Un huh, I know it's God's house," and then they add, "but I still hate to go."

Mothers were girls so they understand girls. They understand how it is to enjoy class projects, fret over clothing and get the chores out of the way. They don't understand boys at all. And since they don't understand them, they nag them, worry over them, and scold them. And they sit back with a shudder and realize it's only a matter of time before the future of the world is in the hands of the likes of their sons.

XXII
This Is the Way
I Iron My Clothes

I dropped in to visit a friend the other day and she was ironing her husband's pajamas. Do you have any idea what that does to a wife who looks for the permanent press label before she looks at the price?

Our kids feel downright disadvantaged when they sing, "This is the way we iron our clothes, iron our clothes," and all that bash in kindergarten. "I thought you ironed in the dryer," one of them told the teacher, and I haven't had the courage to face that particular teacher since. She bought little play irons so all the children would have an opportunity to view them before they became extinct. At least, that's what she told the PTA when she presented the bill for 26 Like Mom irons.

A close relative of mine (put them all together and she spells you-know-who) accused me of never buying anything that won't iron itself inside the dryer. I think that's unfair. I buy things like vinyl raincoats for the kids that are laundered quickly and cheaply with a garden hose. I buy plastic table cloths and only once tried to iron one. I buy clothes with "dry clean only" labels and lots and lots of T-shirts. The day I heard seersucker was coming back was the day I knew the women's movement was having a real impact.

It's wives who iron their husband's pajamas who make it rough on us. "Is he in the hospital?" I asked hopefully. No. "Aha, then it must be convention time for him?" She shook her head. I played my trump hope. "His mother's coming to visit?" I struck out.

She ironed his pjs because he liked them ironed. "Did you ever ask him if he liked them ironed?" No, she admitted, but he never said he didn't like them ironed, and, besides, she'd been ironing them for eighteen years, so he was used to crisp jammies.

Well, I hope they stay together because he's in for a dreadful wrinkle if he ever marries a non-ironer like the wiser of us. I figure that if God wanted us to iron, He wouldn't have given us Permanent Press.

Besides, I discovered that once you start ironing, it starts you on the road to housewifely addiction. Only at the ironing board can you NOT ignore rips that need mending—and buttons that need replacing. (And substandard ironers are known to iron off more buttons than they want to sew on.) Set out to iron one shirt and the evening is shot.

You might argue that what my friend irons is her business but that's not entirely true. Her son may end up marrying my daughter and she will inherit the pain of my sloth. I can hear her now, "What do you mean iron pajamas? Pull up the blanket. Who's to see the wrinkles?"

I can hear him now. "I want my pjs ironed like mother used to iron them."

I can hear her now, "Then take your pajamas to your mother to iron."

I can hear him now, "Hello, Mom, this is Jason. Will you iron my jammies, please?"

I can hear her now, "I knew no good could come from your marriage. You ought to see how her mother never ironed."

I guess I better buy an iron. Just to save my daughter's marriage.

XXIII
Now You Take Camping . . .

. . . And please take it far. Before all you family camping devotees launch into a righteous broadside against my one-sided view of family togetherness, let me be heard.

We've tried camping. Three times. Three nightmares of, "Where's Mike *now*?" Three trips to the emergency room. Three days of laundry. Three bottles of tranquilizers.

I am negative, I admit; but I have but one life to give to my family, and why shorten it on purpose? I like my vacations soft, quiet and in a nice motel where you can pick up a phone and get ice. I don't like them hard, cold and outside where you can pick up a log and get a tick. Let me run through our three experiences at togetherness in the great outdoors before you judge me too harshly.

Trip One: Oldest child five; second child eighteen months; third child out-of-sight; sleeping bags; outdoor fireplace; and hope.

Decided to camp for "just a few days." Stayed overnight. Home by 8 A.M. Reached our mountain retreat "away from it all" thirty minutes after last spot had been taken. Drove around until we found another campground. Tentament City, we dubbed it. Camp spaces closer than we were at home to neighbors. Sounds heavier. Air lighter.

No fireplaces left. Had cold wieners, warm root beer and rain for dinner. Rain also for bedtime. Stuffed wet sleeping bags filled with lively kids in car. Endured it until 5 A.M. Reached home three hours later.

"Did you call off your trip?" neighbors queried.

"Yes," we lied.

Trip Two: Oldest child seven; second child three; third child imminent; tent; camp stove; and determination.

Wiser this time. Decided to try it just for the weekend. Lasted until Saturday noon. Reserved camping spot in advance. It was waiting for us, right next to the outdoor privies. No fresh mountain odor for us. No privacy.

For dinner, picnicked away from our intersection. Hiked fifty yards away to Falling Rock. It did. Ran out of Band-Aids. Had cooked wieners, warm root beer and bruises for dinner. Slept in tent. Every time someone crossed our threshold on his way to the U.S. Forest Service Public Facilities, our kids screamed, "Bear!"

Endured until Saturday A.M.

"What happened?" asked neighbors.

"False labor pains," I lied.

Trip Three and Out: Oldest child eight; second child five; third child home; invited children four, five, seven and nine; cabin; frozen dinners; tranquilizers.

Rented a cabin for a week. Lasted two days. Sleeping bags, giggles, mud, lost children, virus . . . the usual.

We knew when to quit. We've shelved our natural outdoor vacation instincts until our youngest is fifteen.

By that time I will be too old to worry, too tired to chase, and too weak to do anything but watch my family pitch tents, fix fires, cook food, and cater to me.

What? It doesn't work out that way? Well, every mother needs her dream.

XXIV
The Deterioration of an Expert

Monday: I'm awfully glad I'm an expert on children because today I have three of them in the living room sick with something that everybody in school has and which has been keeping them sick in their living rooms for about two weeks.

Tuesday: I'm awfully glad I'm an expert on children and feel free to tell other parents what to do because those of mine who are sick in the living room need sympathy, medicine, and a good swat on the bottom about every twenty minutes.

Thursday: I'm awfully glad I used to consider myself an expert on children because sick children need a good deal of love, patience, and sanity on the part of their mother, and those of mine in the living room are beginning to recuperate much faster than their thermometers show simply because I am ordering it.

Friday: I'm awfully glad that I used to be an expert on children because those two of mine left in the living room still have 101 degree fevers, some leftover candy stashed under the sofa pillows, and one more chance. The other one used his up and is quarantined to the bathroom for the remainder of his convalescence.

Saturday: I'm awfully glad their father is an expert on children because I am leaving the house for the day and their fevers are still negotiable. He has decided to spend a day ministering to them, sympathizing with them, and catching whatever it is that they have.

Monday: I'm awfully glad their father is an ex-expert, too, because as soon as I got back Saturday night and shoveled out the living room, and bound up his psyche, he went to bed with a splitting headache.

Wednesday: I'm awfully glad we don't need experts on children because nobody has any answers for anything unless he has lived through it all, and that one child of mine left in the living room needs a bath, and we've run out of rooms which are being used temporarily as jails.

Friday: I'm awfully glad that I've never claimed to be an expert on children because the past two weeks taught me that a well-balanced mother is vital to the family and that the two are a contradiction in terms. Besides, that kid left in the living room is lonely and wants to know why he doesn't get to spend the day picking locks on the medicine cabinets like the other two.

Sunday: I'm awfully glad there's a Mass obligation. I'm out! I'm out! Never mind the twitches.

Monday: I'm awfully glad the teacher's an expert on children because she gets them today, along with my blessing, my vote for a higher salary, and my sympathy. As for me, I'm going back to being an expert on children again, now that I don't have to have them around. It's the only way to be an expert.

XXV
He Who Sings Maybe Shouldn't

Do you remember when Sister used to pick out three or four kids in the choir and tell them right before the big confirmation Mass that on that one occasion God would like it better if they sang from their hearts instead of their mouths?

Or did you happen to be one of those who "mouthed it" at the Christmas program because the teacher said she needed some big smiles more than big voices?

You weren't fooled, were you? The class knew exactly what she was saying: "Please don't wreck the show with your voice."

Did you ever wonder what happened to the kids who sang from the heart and the kids who mouthed it? Well, we grew up and married each other and gave rise to another generation of tone-deaf singers.

In our efforts during the past decade on getting Catholics to sing at Mass, there's been an emphasis on encouraging everybody to sing. There are the pleas from the lector, "Come on, everyone join us"; and from the guitarists, "We can't hear you out there"; and from the homilists, "He who sings prays twice."

But I haven't heard any instructions on what to do with keeping the non-singer quiet. We are in an uncomfortable situation. If we launch into a lively "What A Great Thing It Is" with feeling, we're apt to inherit the stares of our pew mates. A telltale sign that we're a bit too enthusiastic is when the people in front start turning around, much as we used to do in the olden days, i.e., scratch our necks and grab a quick glance at the choir loft to find out who was doing that terrible singing.

So to avoid that embarrassment, we non-singers tend to shut up. Then we risk looking uncooperative and even belligerent, like some of our fellow worshipers who fold arms and mouths to show their displeasure at having their Mass interrupted by music.

So what do we do? We do what Sr. Choir Director and Second Grade Teacher told us to—we mouth it. The more things change . . .

One of the most embarrassing situations I've found myself in the past couple of years grew out of my lack of singing ability. I was a speaker at a diocesan workshop that culminated in a highly participatory episcopal Mass. When I read the program for the Mass, I began to shake. Each speaker was to sing a verse of the Beatitudes from the microphone and the congregation was to sing a response.

I considered an earlier flight, laryngitis, and defiance, but I settled for honesty. "I can't sing," I explained, but they wouldn't believe me.

"You did such a good job with your workshop."

"But I can't sing," I held on. They finally and reluctantly let me off but it just added one more mystery to the problem of what to do with the non-singer in today's liturgy. Why don't people believe you when you tell them you can't sing? Why are they bent on your proving it publicly?

Come to think of it, I can't ever remember hearing a tone-deaf priest sing High Mass in the olden days. What happened to the priest who couldn't sing? Maybe we need an organization.

XXVI
Suburban Speedway:
Shopping Center Parking Lots

My husband contends that the freeway is the most dangerous stretch of highway in America but that's only because he doesn't drive the supermarket parking lots. For sheer thrills, you can't beat them.

I don't mean to one-up Evel Knievel, but sometimes I envy him, driving straight through the air in a cycle unhampered by groceries, kids, manned carts, runaway carts, and motorists bearing down on one empty parking space, oblivious to the drivers around them.

There may be a special set of driving rules for supermarket parking lots but I haven't been able to locate them. In vain I searched through the state Motor Vehicle Division's *Facts for Drivers and Pedestrians* but it contains no rules governing parking lots.

"Supermarket parking lots are private property, so we can't enforce normal driving regulations," a uniformed driving regulator told me, and then had the naiveté to add, "I'll tell you this, though. They're a big headache." More like a migraine, officer.

Still, women seem to accept the challenge with equanimity. Last Thanksgiving I witnessed a supermarket scene that seemed to put it all in perspective. A mother who had dropped her teenage daughter off to begin the shopping while she parked, came in casually and said to the girl, "I just hit a car. Go ahead and finish the shopping and get in line, okay? Oh—and Honey, see if you can get a twelve-pound hen instead of a tom turkey, okay?"

A few minutes later, I heard the manager ask for the owner of a blue Chevy. Still later, when I wheeled my pushcart out, I passed the two women, the hitter and the hittee, exchanging the names of their insurance agents.

Just as I pushed by, I heard the errant driver confide to her victim, "Well, to be honest, I can relax now. I've had my annual fender bash." The other woman nodded understandingly.

Why do people who are careful and considerate drivers on the streets and highways turn into maniacs in supermarket parking lots? In researching this article, I asked two driver training teachers if they ever took their students into the big parking lots for practice. "Not on your life," they said in unison, their eyes big as cash register tabs.

"Why not?" I asked.

"Because they're not ready for defensive driving. They need stop lights and signals, turning lanes and courtesy. You don't find those in the parking lots. *We* don't even like to drive there."

So, I had unearthed two causes of parking lot mayhem: no rules and no practice. But it wasn't until I talked to a cart caddy that the light bulbs really flashed. We were zig-zagging our way to my car when I asked him if he witnessed many near accidents.

"Three today, one hit," he replied. Then his eyes brightened in memory. "Day before Christmas was our biggest day—nine cars."

"Why do you suppose people drive like that in supermarket parking lots?" I asked.

"They drive out here just like they do in there," he replied, nodding toward the store.

Of course, that was it! Parking lot driving is just part of the whole supermarket experience. The woman who plunges her cart against a tide of shoppers heading west is also the woman who lunges her car against traffic in the lot. And the man who barges in front of you at the check-out line is the man who takes the parking space away from you as you're heading into it.

Perhaps we need to begin with driving rules inside the store: four-way stop signs at the produce bins, one way north on the pet food aisle, south on soaps, and crosswalk lines in front of the meat counter. Turning signals for carts are long overdue.

But until we reorient our cart drivers, we have to face the real danger outside the store. In the absence of any written rules and regulations, I venture to offer a few:

Right-of-Way: The right-of-way in supermarket parking lots should not be confused with the right-of-way in other driving situations. Generally speaking, the right-of-way belongs to:

1A: The driver who is there already, or

1B. The most dented car, or

1C. The housewife in the biggest rush to beat the kids home, or

1D. The car with most frozen food in it.

Pedestrian Safety: At the supermarket, as elsewhere, the pedestrian always has the right-of-way unless:

2A. She looks as though she will wait.

2B. She has small children attached.

2C. She does not want to get splashed.

Method of Signaling:

3A. Index finger pointed straight indicates dibs on that parking space.

3B. Eyes frozen front indicates refusal to grant parking space or right-of-way.

3C. Fingers tapping on steering wheel means driver is triple parking only long enough for wife to buy a loaf of bread, a six pack and a pound of ground beef.

3D. Chin resting on palm attached to elbow resting on car door indicates extreme disgust with other driver's boorishness. (For best reaction, see 3B.)

3E. Familiar thumb signal usually indicates, "Put the groceries back there," and should not be interpreted as a back-up signal.

Driving Patterns: Any hole, go.

Traffic Markings: Yellow boxes indicate parking lots for the carts; solid white lines, broken yellow lines and other symbolic designs suggest driving patterns and parking spots; however, since general usage dictates otherwise, flexible driving is encouraged.

Leaving a Parked Position: The proper procedure for leaving a parked position is to put the car in Park, open the door, and remove all grocery carts standing behind rear tires; then, cautiously allow yourself to be nudged out by the car heading in the opposite space, while swiveling head from front to back and side to side, simultaneously signaling to the waiting driver behind you that you must have the space in which he is idling in order to back up.

Moving Violations: Commonly called grocery carts, these runaways frequently confuse drivers, particularly if there's a strong wind. As many as six fast-rolling carts have been spotted driverless in one parking lot, causing untold havoc. Proper procedure is to stop the car, allow the cart right-of-way, and report any minor collisions. Supermarkets generally ask repair costs only.

I've passed over some of the stranger situations like getting tangled up with Goodwill boxes, photo developing cabins and a bicycle lane in one suburb that ran smack through a parking lot, but I'm saving those for another article to be entitled *Creative Nervous Breakdown*.

XXVII
If I Should Die Before I Wake!

One of the worst fears we ever willed upon a child was the prayer, "Now I lay me down to sleep," with its insidious phrase, "If I should die before I wake."

"If I should die before I wake." What kind of loving confidence is that supposed to instill in the poor child who knows that within a few seconds the light will go out and he'll be left with the "ghoulies and ghosties and things that go bump in the night."

And to children there are still things that go bump in the night. They see them. They hear them and they fear them. Our first tendency, to laugh off their fears and fancies, doesn't help any more than it helps to laugh off an older person's fear of noises in the dark. Adults, after all, are just grownup kids and they have their own nocturnal nervousness pretty well established.

Many parents want to help a child overcome fear of night. How can they do it? By eliminating their own fears, for a start, or by concealing them from the children. Anyone who has ever lain awake hearing noises in the dark and lonely night knows how one's imagination can get carried away. A creaking tree branch, through the process of fear and fantasy, can escalate into a legion of marauders bent on dastardly deeds. Fears fertilize and grow in the night.

To show the extreme that adult fears can reach,

there's the case a few years back where a man sued his wife for divorce because of her unreasonable fear of the dark. So convinced was she that she might sleep through a possible intruder, she sprinkled corn flakes in the hallway outside their bedroom door, resolving thus to hear the crunch of unwanted persons.

Instead, her husband trod the cereal in bare feet while putting the cat out and she never woke, either then or during the time it took him to extract the sharp bits of flakes from his tender soles. He was awarded the divorce.

How else can we prevent rearing future corn flake sprinklers? We can listen to our kids' fears. What is it that frightens them most when the lights go out? With one of ours, we discovered that the shadows that the night light produced on the chair backs and chandelier made her believe that there were dinosaurs in the dining room.

We darkened the house, turned on the night light and saw it as she pointed out. Sure enough, the shadows etched a grotesque dinosaur along the east wall which she had to face in traveling from her room to the bath. We changed the location of the night light and our dinosaur became extinct. Then we all laughed about it, but not before.

With another child, it was even funnier. One night after the water softener left its usual gift of air in the pipes, Mike decided he wanted a drink. "I went into the bathroom and turned on the faucet and it sounded like it was shooting me, so I ran out and decided to go the back bathroom to get a drink. Just when I got in front of the refrigerator, it turned on and scared me. So I ran back into bed and put my pillow over my head and pretended I wasn't thirsty."

So we turned out all the lights and listened to the faucet and the refrigerator together.

We should understand, too, that fears in the night are a composite of those poured into us during the day. Allowing kids to watch scary shows, whether it's just before bed or early in the morning, takes its toll in night-time security. Too often nightmares are based on daymares.

Still, our best solution came out of one of our kids, the same one whose head landed under the pillow. He sleeps in a room with his three-year-old brother who had a monster on his ceiling. We tried to talk Steve out of his monster, turning out lights and saying, "See, it isn't there." It didn't work. He still saw it. Sometimes he didn't want to go into his room in the dark to get a book because of the monster.

Then, suddenly, we stopped hearing about the monster. Curious, we asked Steve if it didn't frighten him any longer. "Oh, it's gone," he said. "Mike shot it."

And Mike had. He saw the problem and killed it. This satisfied Steve. (We could have done that with the dinosaur, I suppose.) I'd like to think it was brotherly love that did it, but I rather suspect the monster was beginning to get to Mike, too. After all, they slept in the same room with it.

XXVIII
A Letter to Grandma

Dear Mom:

9 A.M. Can you believe I've got a whole day without any appointments, meetings or even cooking? The kids are off to school. I cleaned house yesterday and we're having leftovers tonight. I am going to spend the entire day at my desk, catching up on letters and then starting on the outline of my book.

I'm beginning to get polite reminders from my editor noting that the first draft was due a few months ago. The book is going to be about—

(10:30)—Well, that didn't last long. Anne's car broke down so I had to rescue the pre-schoolers and deliver them to school. Then drive Anne to her husband's office to get their other car.

As long as I was out, I figured I might as well pick up some cleaning and stop off for a book they were holding for me at the library. Walked in and saw at least three people I knew and they all had something important to tell me.

I just couldn't ignore Marcy. I think I wrote you about her. She has the husband who—

(1 P.M.)—Guess who got interrupted again! Harry surprised me by coming home for lunch. Had forgotten an important paper he needed for a meeting, and since he had to return home sometime today to get it, he

decided he'd meet me for lunch—in front of the refrigerator. There went tonight's leftovers and a letter or two.

But it was pleasant being able to lunch and talk together without interruptions from those perfect grandchildren of yours. Oops, doorbell.

(2:15)—That was some kind of FBI man doing a check on one of the neighbors who needs a security clearance to make tires for missiles or something. Rather humorless guy. When he asked me if I knew of any reason the neighbor shouldn't be cleared, I said, "Well, his dog barks all the time." He didn't twitch a whisker and actually wrote it down! Gads. I hope he doesn't credit that bit of levity to me.

Oh, oh, kids are home. Will get their snacks and be right back.

(4 P.M.)—Forgot Henrietta had an orthodontist appointment. Dropped the boys off at CCD on the way and hope to finish this letter before—

(9 P.M.)—Well, just re-read this letter and it doesn't make much sense. It was so nice having a day just to myself but I didn't fill you in on the really important news. Sorry but I think I'll mail it anyway. I don't have another day off until a week from Thursday and today I got another letter from my editor. If I don't get him the outline by the end of the month, he's going to ask for my advance back. I've already spent it on a new sewing machine. Two months ago. Haven't used it yet but it sure is pretty.

Love,
Your daughter

XXIX
The Leftovers-for-Lunch Bunch

One of the tragedies of today's television commercials is that the have-nots in this country actually think we live the way that the advertisers pretend we do. After seeing hundreds of commercials of middle-class housewives beautifully coiffured, manicured, and figured, with little to do besides chase white knights or birds or what-have-you out of their immaculate kitchens, the poor have come to believe that this is the way the other people really live.

How can we blame them? (Directly after the Watts riot, one small boy told an interviewer that he had seen a commercial of a white man carrying his money to the bank in a wheelbarrow because he had so much. "I thought if I helped him, he'd maybe give me some," said the boy.)

I don't know if it will do much good, but I'd like to suggest a movement toward realistic commercials depicting home life. Here is my platform for a starter.

—Prohibit all laundry product commercials where the housewives compare soaps. I've never yet heard any two women so bereft of conversation that they must discuss whiteners, bluings, and suds. Along with this, prohibit the easy-going, laundry-day conversations over the washer or the fence. Substitute hectic scenes of disheveled mothers in shifts glancing anxiously up at the sky to see if the rain will beat the smog to the clothesline or waiting at the drier for Suzie's tennis shoes so she can make it to kindergarten on time.

—Abolish all those leisurely housewife coffee get-togethers in which there is a silver coffee service and cups with saucers. Substitute mugs half-filled with left-over breakfast coffee and surreptitiously sipped as mothers rest from getting half their family off to school and eye the other half, wondering what to do with it all day.

—Do away with those horrible breakfast scenes where the clean and happy little boy offers his mom his cereal to give her pep all day. Make it more realistic with each child hugging his favorite cereal possessively and mother prying it out of his arms with the promise that he can have the empty box when the cereal is gone. Add a few motherly comments like, "You picked it out—you eat it," and "No, you can't have sugar on sugared cereal." Set aside forty-five minutes after breakfast for cutting out, fighting over, putting to-gether, filling out, and breaking cereal premiums. Oh, yes, don't forget the scene with the alphabet cereal where the kids race to put their names together with soggy letters, trading and squabbling, as mother learns to live with another eccentric headache.

Compare this breakfast scene with the typical happy family one on television where Dad, Mom, and the All-American kids munch and agree on one cereal. Pre-posterous! (As a matter of fact, I can't think of a father I know who endures the family breakfast trial in the first place.)

—Away, too, with all those gay commercials where Mom greets her muddy son with glee because she has a new detergent. Any mother worth her washboard is going to groan and say, "*Where* did you get that mud? Hose yourself down before you come in—and why didn't you wear your boots?"

Boycott all products which Boob The Clown tells the kiddies, "Go ask your Mommy to get you one right away at your friendly Fiction Factory." The only relief from these crass commercials is that there are so many of them that the kids get them all mixed up and can't remember what to ask you for by the end of the program. Or else they run to the kitchen to tell you each time, and I suppose that has a physical fitness advantage. The kids eventually become immune to these pleas. One of ours came to us once and said, "The man said you're supposed to get me a civil defense test right away."

—Get rid of Mrs. Olson and concentrate on shaping up the husband instead of the coffee. When he gripes about the coffee, have the cute little wife blink her eyes and say, "But, darling, this is tea," or "What can you expect from a Phi Beta Kappa, honey?"

—Finally, get rid of those lovely lunch commercials where the menu is planned in detail, the table daintily set, and the family-at-home gathered together to try new delicacies. No honest-to-goodness mother has any idea of what's for lunch until she opens the refrigerator door. She smorgasbords all those little dabs of leftovers and doles them out according to seniority—of both food and children. Sometimes she makes an heroic effort to camouflage leftovers of some antiquity by dousing them with catsup or mixing them together, but kids are getting more perceptive every day.

That ends my platform for more honest commercials. If we're going to portray middle-class life, let's not pretend that we live in a world of sterile gadgets, children, and teapots. Let's show it the way it is—noisy, cluttered, and homey. Then maybe even we would start believing the television commercials.

XXX
"I Didn't Do It."
"I Didn't Do It."
"Neither Did I."

I want to get in on the exorcism fad before it's all written up. Suddenly, it seems as though everyone is talking about demonology and the strange inexplicable behaviors of things around the house.

Well, quite frankly, I welcome an explanation like that. We've had inexplicable activity around this house for some time. And I'm chagrined to admit I've blamed the family, even though they've vigorously denied it.

For a long time, for instance, my scissors have taken to disappearing. I accused one child and then another, particularly after finding the scissors in: (1) their beds, (2) their dresser drawers, or (3) their model airplane kits. But they always denied having anything to do with taking them out of their designed nest and not putting them back. Now it is clear that some kind of mischievous spirit is at work here, removing the scissors and placing them in weird places. It's nice to know the kids are innocent.

And then there's the mystery of the chandelier socks. About every other week, the light fixture in our sons' room starts sprouting socks—first a red one, size 8, followed by a blue one, a bit smaller, and so on. "How did that sock get up there?" I asked Son One sternly.

"I don't know," he replied in whites-of-eyes innocence.

"Were you kicking it up in the air to make a chandelier basket again?"

"Oh, no," he shook his innocent little locks. "I just woke up this morning and saw that sock hanging there."

The next day saw two more socks there, and his little brother insisted he had nothing to do with it. "Besides," he added naively, "I can only kick mine as far as the window sill."

I confess I disbelieved them. I thought they were having contests to see who could shoot the dirty socks the highest and make a direct hit on the light fixture. It's a relief to know some malevolent spirit does it instead and that my children remain innocent.

Disappearing soda-pop, cookies and candy constituted another mistaken idea of mine that perhaps my innocent offspring were not quite so innocent at times. When I discovered rich brown crumbs all over my son's face or pillow and the last half-dozen Oreo cookies missing, I tended to question his vow that he hadn't touched the cookie jar. Now I take comfort in the idea that some hungry spirit eats those cookies and leaves the crumbs on my children's faces.

It's encouraging to know, in fact, that all those things that formerly met with the protest, "I didn't do it," are now explicable. The devil makes them do it.

The devil got an early start this morning by leaving a few raisins under the wheels of my typing chair. I hardly traveled eight round trips between desk and typewriter before I was grounded in raisin quicksand on the hardwood floor of my office.

I called all three innocents into my office and pointed

to the evidence. "Who dropped raisins under the wheels and didn't pick them up?"

"I didn't."

"I didn't."

"I didn't."

I smelled each one's breath for *parfum au raisin* and dug out my magnifying glass to peer under fingernails. I chose the one reeking of evidence, turned him around and gave him a solid reminder of the backside.

Then I looked into his eyes innocently and said, "I didn't do that."

He was outraged. "You did, too . . . then who did it?" through tearful pupils.

"The devil made me do it," I said. I think I'm going to like this demonology kick.

XXXI
Year-Round School
Equals Year-Round Family

At times the idea of year-round school appeals to me, and at other times it doesn't. On Sunday nights, New Year's Day, and August 30, it's the best idea ever. But when I think of having the equivalent of Christmas vacation every nine weeks, I get the holiday hives all over again.

To lay the groundwork for a discussion on the advantages and disadvantages of year-round school, I'll set forth a scandalous basic premise: most mothers dislike having children around the house all day.

Before I'm taken apart by super-patient mothers who really are scandalized to hear another mother admit she likes peace and serenity a few hours a day, let me scurry to add that I love my children. I love them in the morning until about 9 A.M. and I love them in the afternoon after 3:30. The hours in-between I love my preschooler, who gets a chance to finish a sentence when the others buzz off.

I don't think I'm alone in this, either. I've seen quite a few PTA-types cowering in the supermarket in late August, squeezing the avocados just to stall going home to "There's nuthin' to do . . ." and "Jamie looked at me." I've met more than one friend volunteering to stuff envelopes after they've had a siege of flu at home. No other mother questions their devotion.

Where is it written that husbands can freely admit they don't want wives and children in their offices and children can admit they don't want parents at school but mothers can't admit they don't like having husbands and children at home between nine and three? What are our office hours? Where can we go to be away from those near and dear to us?

Back in my pre-parent days, I remember reading somebody's (was it St. Thomas) five proofs of God, but since I've become a mother of school-aged children, I've developed five more obvious proofs of God's love: (1) Monday morning; (2) bedtime; (3) September; (4) 98.6; and (5) the part-time job.

Each of these gives the child the opportunity to discover God's goodness out there in the world and the mother the opportunity to discover it at home.

Now that I've practically admitted heresy, let's go on to year-round school. The system that's most popular around these parts is the 45-15 system, or forty-five days of school followed by fifteen days of vacation year round. Nine weeks on, three weeks off.

For the mother, it boils down to exchanging the horrors of August for the week after Christmas four times a year. So, in terms of sanity, it remains equal *unless* . . .

And it's that unless that bothers me. "Unless the school is unable to coordinate children's quarters" is the way the brochure runs. What it's saying is that a mother could conceivably have one child entering his three weeks off and another starting it. That's six weeks of refrigerator-to-TV child four times a year. Even August is better.

Let's say the school is able to coordinate it so the kids

can be home the same three weeks to fight together. What with the various epidemics and viruses incubating year-round, our schedule could look like a mother's nightmare: four weeks of school, one week of tonsillitis, four weeks of school, three weeks off, three weeks of school, one week of flue, six weeks of school, three weeks off. And that's only one child!

What's the answer? Well, since I basically agree with the idea of breaking up education for the emotional health of children and I am familiar with the tenuous emotional health of mothers, how about a compromise?

Let's have year-round school, doing away with three months every summer, but instead of the three weeks off every nine weeks, let's just subtract the time the kids are sick or at the orthodontists and eye factory.

If number one child has a bout of tonsillitis and a stubbed toe (requiring him to miss two days of school because his shoes don't fit), let's subtract these days from his three weeks off. If numbers two, three, and four children get the chicken pox, that's their vacation, take it or leave it.

Granted, it might create havoc with the computer and it might not promote the best mental health for teachers but it's bound to result in happier mothers and healthier children. It's either that or eliminating August. Imagine the confusion that would cause.

XXXII
Boycotting the Tooth Fairy

A friend of mine was the perfect mother in all ways but one. She kept forgetting to pay off the tooth fairy.

Every so often a child whose mouth resembled an IBM card woke wailing: "The tooth fairy forgot again."

Filled with guilt, my friend suggested quickly that he put the tooth back under the pillow to try again. That evening she doubled the ante, and when he woke the following morning, he was delighted.

After this went on a couple of years, one of her daughters confided to the family at breakfast: "Boy, that tooth fairy sure is dumb. I keep shoving the same teeth back under the pillow and she keeps paying me for them."

Yes, Virginia, there is a tooth fairy. And whatever parent dreamed her up deserves her. I strongly suspect it wasn't a parent at all but some desperate dentist who wanted to make an extraction attractive, so he told the child the tooth was worth more out of his mouth than in. Once the idea took hold, greed took over.

Inflation has hit the tooth fairy. My second grade sources tell me the going rate for a lost tooth is now twenty-five cents. I won't pay it. Ten cents and no more. Well, maybe fifteen but that's my limit . . . unless, of course, Jimmy's fairy pays more and my child wails: "The tooth fairy likes Jimmy better'n me."

My daughter announced proudly at Show and Tell a few years back that she had a dime from the tooth fairy, and half the class snorted, "Only a dime? Boy, you must have creepy teeth."

We seem destined to continually exhibit mouths in various stages of gap. I sometimes wonder if we'll ever all be able to smile on the same Christmas card. When our four-year-old finally got his two-year molars he watched enviously as his sister lost a tooth a week. She was much more financially independent those toothless days.

When our baby got his first tooth years ago, what was their first comment? "When will he lose it?" With each new tooth, he became more valuable. They studied this new source which was to be harvestable in five years and wondered how best to exploit him.

Meanwhile, we keep paying. If the rate keeps going up, we're going to have to cut down on our dental visits. There are alternatives. One mother plants a quarter per tooth but insists that her children spend it for tooth-paste. That's clever.

Another uses the Peter Pan technique. If the child doubts the existence of the fairy, she stops paying. When the child complains, she says innocently: "Well, there must have been some mistake. She always brings money to those who believe." The child swears to an undying belief until the tooth fairy skips him again. Then he tells every toddler within miles that there isn't any tooth fairy.

One mother told me that her eleven-year-old still believed in the tooth fairy. "Oh, she doesn't *really* believe, does she?" I said.

"Yes," replied the mother. "And she'll believe for two more years, according to my sun signs."

As I said, some parents deserve the tooth fairy.

XXXIII
Column Revisited

One of the thrills in an author's life comes from hearing his own material quoted by someone who doesn't know he's the author. This happened to me last March in San Francisco.

I had nagged my husband, Jim, into letting me tag along to his convention. Since I had some West Coast interviews I wanted to do, it worked out beautifully.

We went exploring San Francisco on foot one Sunday morning and ended up at the site of the then new and unopened cathedral. Around the corner, in a school serving as temporary cathedral, Mass was just starting, so, we went in.

When the priest began his homily with, "For my sermon, I'm going to use a clipping from the *Denver Register* sent to me by a friend," Jim and I exchanged glances. When he went on to read my column, "The Children Listened," our mouths opened wide.

Who could put together a series of coincidences like that? Here I was, a thousand miles from home sitting in a temporary church which we just happened to stumble upon when Mass was beginning, hearing my own words. It was a strange sensation.

But stranger was the dissimilarity between the scene of the writing and the scene of the listening. I remember doing that column. I had a sick baby, two or three neighborhood children, a nagging phone, and a cold. I would write a couple of lines, answer the phone, scratch those lines, wipe a nose, write new lines, settle a fight and quit. A few minutes later, I'd start it over, telling myself, "Now, this is a good idea. Get with it."

As I sat there listening to my own words coming from the pulpit, I reconstructed the afternoon they were written. It went like this:

He fasted from meat . . .

("Mom, Stevie's crying." Checked it out. Routine sandbox fight. Listened to both sides, all versions, and handed down verdict. No more sandbox for anybody. Back to column.)

. . . on Friday.

She cooked meat . . .

(Phone. "This is Disabled Veterans calling. Our truck will be in your neighborhood tomorrow . . ." "Thank you!" Back to column.)

. . . on Friday.

Their children . . .

(Feverish baby ambled in, held up arms, needed loving. Forty-five minutes and two baby aspirins later, he fell asleep. Back to typewriter.)

. . . looked at each other.

He said the nuns' habits . . .

(Knock. Neighbor, "Heard you had a sick baby. Can I do anything?" "Thank you! Nice of you." Back to column.)

. . . were too short . . .

("Holy cow! Got to get the roast in." Half-hour later, back at desk.)

. . . for respectability.

("Hi. I'm home. What's for snack? Can I play at Libby's?")

This kind of day isn't peculiar to me. Any mother will recognize it for what it is—a day-long interruption.

That's why it seemed so ludicrous to me, sitting in such a hushed atmosphere hearing my words as if they had been written in a peaceful study with soundproof walls, soft music and a strong lock.

As it was, when I heard those words coming from the pulpit, I was pleased. I was also tense, anticipating any minute a wail and "Mom, he did it again!"

XXXIV
My Children
Don't Understand Me

I've been accused of disliking the junior high aged child, an accusation I've fought with a tenacity. I gave two years of my sanity to teaching eighth grade English, a feat I hope is duly recorded in the purgatory ledgers.

I followed that with an eternity of seventh grade CCD—usually girls usually giggling—and I emerged from that experience with the suspicion that while God didn't make many mistakes, early adolescence was his biggie.

I suspect it wasn't really an oversight on his part, creating an unidentifiable bundle of emotions and energy to test authority and test it and test it and . . .

But, rather, it was an intentional madness. As the saying goes, he gave us cuddly little babies to love and nurture, and then turned them into tyrants so we'd be glad to release them to society.

Trying to judge God's motives, however, is less useful than coming up with a way to cope with pubescent offspring. After much experience with OPC (Other People's Children), I'm now getting my come-uppance at home. Crises come but never seem to go. Spirits are high one moment, lower than a boy's grades the next.

My spirits react accordingly, and life in the kitchen resembles that eighth grade classroom of twenty years ago.

I can hear you now, "*You* at least knew what you were getting into. *You* knew what they were like. We came into it cold."

True, but what expectant parent expects anything but a baby? I was too excited about tiny fingers to even think about pierced ears or what "all the other girls do."

Now, after some reflection, I believe I've come up with a method for smoothing parent-early teen relationships. Our emphasis has been on the parents' need to understand their adolescent. If only we listened, if only we understood peer pressure, if only we were there when they needed us, all would go well.

Let's reconsider that folly and put the education where it belongs—teach the kids to understand us. Let's blanket the media, the schools, and the institutions with the message: *Children, take time to understand your parents. Listen to them when they want to talk.* (Even if it means pulling your ear plug.)

Hear what your parents are saying. ("I squeezed into your room today," and "Who's paying the phone bill anyway?")

Try to understand your parents are in their difficult years. ("Will I lose my job?" "Should I go to work?" "When will their feet stop growing?")

Don't expect too much of your parents. (Only saints can be in two places at once. Only saints can divine that you'll be in a different mood five minutes from now. And good old St. Dad doesn't function well after a pajama party.)

Be loyal to your parents. (No reasonable offspring would discuss parents with the gang. Never!)

Finally, *love your parents in spite of their faults.* (It's the only one that makes any sense.)

XXXV
Questions Parents Ask

I was folding laundry one day when the kids came home from school. Seeing my hands busy and my mind vacant, they decided to chat a bit. Sara started it off with, "Well, what did you learn at home today?"

I stopped in mid-diapers. Her intonation was an exact replica of mine, even down to the maternal smile which accompanies that question when I ask it of her. I searched her face to see if she was trying to be funny. She wasn't.

She was taking her cue from me in starting an after-school conversation. Usually I asked her, "What did you learn in school today?" and she was turning tables.

What did I learn? I asked myself. Well, for one thing, I learned not to ask that question again.

What did I learn? Well, I learned that it didn't do any good to ask the water softener man to knock before entering. He still barged in, scaring the wits out of me. A valuable bit of discovery . . .

And, let's see, I learned that toddler Steve loved cottage cheese last night but hated it today. Why? Surely that should lead me into some exciting research. . .

I learned that a woman in Reading, Pennsylvania hated my column on being a perfect parent and that a man in Riverside, California loved it. Since one letter neutralized the other, I learned nothing.

I couldn't think of a single reasonable answer. Oh, I had learned some things but they sounded too silly to voice. So I bribed the kids with a cookie and found a conversational base away from what any of us learned that day.

Since then, I've kept my ears open to some of the more vapid questions we ask our children, questions we expect them to answer seriously. Let's put ourselves in their sneakers for a bit. How would we answer the questions we ask?

Imagine yourself five minutes late for an orthodontist appointment. You have the patient in the car, you grab your coat and reach for the car keys. Not there. You search three purses, two dressers and the baby. Finally, you exclaim frantically to your waiting child, "I can't find my car keys."

Her face registers proper concern and she asks helpfully, "Where did you lose them?"

Or, Dad (you're not immune to this business of asking foolish questions), how about this one? You're watching the Big Game, the semi-finals of the final pre-postseason showdown, and your team is behind by three points in the last two minutes. One of your men intercepts a pass and has a clear road ahead to the goal line. You jump up excitedly, ready to shout in triumph when . . . he trips.

That's right. He just trips and lies there for all the world to see. Instead of cheering, you kick the hassock clear across the carpet.

Your five-year-old son looks up and asks indignantly, "Whatever made you do that, young man?"

Well, you've got the idea, but in case I didn't mention your favorite, here are a few more parental games.

"Who do you think you are?" and/or "Who do you think I am?"

"Did I hear you correctly?"

"Why did you tattle?" and/or "Why didn't you tell me?"

"Whatever possessed you . . .?"

"Why would anyone . . .?"

"What do you mean, 'How come'?"

Still, there's no need to beat ourselves to a hair shirt for asking foolish questions occasionally. Just take a look at the kids' answers. Not long ago, I asked a child of mine, "Whatever possessed you to spend good money for that?"

"It wasn't good money," he replied. "It was old money."

Come to think of it, "What did you learn in school today?" isn't such a bad question after all.

XXXVI
Old Is . . .

Old is reading that the high schoolers are having a Fabulous Fifties dance and wearing old-fashioned clothes.

Old is mentioning that your hall closet is a Fibber McGee closet and being the only one in the room who knows what it is.

Old is saying, "the War" and everyone asks, "Which war?"

Old is having a baby when your roommate in the hospital tells you her mother is your age.

Old is remembering when you bought the family groceries for $13 a week.

Old is having a mother's helper but recalling that she used to be called a hired girl.

Old is how you feel when somebody tells you nostalgia is dangerous.

Old is being able to recall the hue and cry against the crew cut when it came in.

Old is remembering a time when you didn't know a divorced person.

Old is how you feel when your children ask you if they had hospitals when you were born.

Old is knowing people who lost children to strep throat a generation or two ago.

Old is a reality every time you say, "When I was your age . . ."

Old is telling your wide-eyed daughter about filling up your dance card with potential dates at the prom.

Old is mentioning that you didn't have to fight off boys at a drive-in theater because they didn't have drive-in theaters then.

Old is remembering when people talked about women who dyed their hair.

Old is explaining to your kids what Lent used to be like.

Old is recalling the time that four children were considered a small family.

Old is how you feel when they ask you at the kindergarten Spring song fest if you want to sit with the mothers or the grandmothers.

Old is trying on your wedding dress and crying at how it has shrunk.

Old is feeling peppy and ready to attack the world each morning until about 9 A.M.

Old is not having to impress people anymore, not trying to look eighteen anymore, and not having all the answers anymore.

Old is comfortable.

XXXVII
Parental Backfires

The road to parenthood is paved with backfires, and if we can't learn from other parents' experiences, at least we can enjoy them. In truth, I feel a lot better knowing that other people's children show occasional bits of irreverence, illiteracy and other non-hereditary traits.

* * * * *

A religion teacher who was preparing her children for reception of First Communion asked her students to write out the question they would most like to ask God if they could. She expected questions such as "When will I die?" and "Will I go to heaven?" and other weighty queries.

However, the question that bothered most of her students was technical: "God, how do you keep from falling out of heaven?"

* * * * *

Then there was the family that was planning a trip to France, so the parents asked the teacher of Tom, 5, to show him France on the globe and maps to better familiarize him with it.

When they reached France, Tom was obviously disappointed.

* * * * *

And there was the time the priest visited religion class and talked with the children about sin. "What happens if you die in a state of mortal sin?" he asked a girl.
"You go to confession, Father."
"But whom would you confess to in hell?"
"You, Father," she replied.

* * * * *

And, like most parents who try the roundabout way of behavior modification once, a mother got caught introducing fibbing into a casual conversation with her daughter. After a few minutes of talk, the girl looked her straight in the eye and asked, "Are you scolding me or just talking about it?"
"Just talking about it," fibbed her mother.

* * * * *

And I can't forget the mother who washed her son's mouth out with soap and he acquired a taste for it. After that she had to stash the soap away to keep him from nibbling on it.

* * * * *

There was also the teacher who, upon discovering most of the girls in her class wished they had been born boys, gave them stories of famous women to build a pride in their own sex. Still, there remained one girl who steadfastly wished she were a boy.

"Why is it you want so badly to be a boy?" the teacher asked.

"Because then I wouldn't have to marry one when I grow up."

* * * * *

We pass a little cemetery on our way to the shopping center. When our daughter was four or so, she asked us, "What are all those little bricks for?"

We explained that they were headstones for people who died. She nodded in understanding.

A year and many trips past that spot later, she said in puzzlement, "You know, I can see how they get bodies into those big stones, but how do they scrunch them up into those little ones?"

XXXVIII
How Parents Stay Humble

Ah, well, so it goes. A mother in Atlanta tells me the true story of a friend of hers, also a mother. It seems that the kids begged for a hamster, and after the usual fervent vows that they alone would care for it, they got it. They named it Danny.

Two months later, when Mom found herself official gamekeeper, responsible for feeding, cleaning and cussing the little varmint, she found a home for it and waited for the kids to come home from school so she could break the news of Danny's imminent departure to them.

They took it much better than she had expected. One of them protested, "But he's been around here a long time. We'll miss him."

To which Mom replied, "Yes, but he's too much work for one person, and since I'm that one person, I say he goes."

Another child offered plaintively, "Well, maybe if he wouldn't eat so much and wouldn't be so messy, we could keep him."

"Uh uh," replied Mom in her no-argue voice. "I've found a good home for him, and he's going before his new owners change their minds."

So the kids turned their attention to their snacks. It was after snack time that it all exploded. "It's time to take Danny to his new home now," said Mom. "Go get his cage."

With one voice and in tearful outrage the children shouted, "Danny! We thought you said Daddy!"

So it goes, fellow parents.

And then there's the mother-turned-religion teacher in Helena who tells me that she and her students worked strenuously on role-playing the Annunciation-Visitation story of Mary to play for the parents. All went according to script until the actual night of the production.

When a travel-weary Mary knocked at the door of her cousin, Elizabeth, the latter answered, not with "Hail" or joyful surprise, but rather with, "Well, so what? I'm pregnant, too."

So it goes, fellow parents. Keep trying.

And there's the conscientious mother who taught her children their grace and Pledge of Allegiance as soon as they could verbalize, only to hear them ending the daily grace like this: "Bless us, O Lord, for these Thy gifts which we are about to receive with liberty and justice for all." Amen, partners in parenthood.

And we can't forget the dad who, trying to offset the grief of his young son over the death of his favorite little turtle, suggested a full funeral. Together they dug the plot, made a tombstone, lined a box with velvet and processed solemnly out the back door. At this point, the turtle moved slightly. The boy looked at the turtle, then at the anticipated funeral, and said to his dad, "Let's kill him."

Finally, there's this mother who, full with child, told her young daughter about the blessed event about to hit the family but asked her not to tell Little Brother that

Mommy was carrying a baby, because the time would seem so long to him. A few days later, Little Brother asked, "When are you going to the hospital to have that rabbit?"

"Rabbit?" shrieked this mother.

Little Daughter explains, "I knew you didn't want him to know about the baby so I told him you were going to have a rabbit." Naturally, he was disappointed.

So it goes, fellow parents, but stay in there. I understand there's a lot more to come.